WORLD OF VOCABULARY

ORANGE

Sidney J. Rauch   Zacharie J. Clements

Assisted by Barry Schoenholz

D1158559

GLOBE BOOK COMPANY, INC.

A Division of Simon & Schuster

New York/Cleveland/Toronto/Sydney/Tokyo/Singapore

PHOTO CREDITS

Page 2, 5, 7, 32, 35, 37, 38, 41, 43, 44, 50, 53, 55, 56, 59, 68, 71, 73, 74, 79, 86, 91, 103, 110, 116, 119: UPI/The Bettmann Archive; 8, 11: Ron Galella; 13: Photofest; 14: © 1989 John H. Cornell Jr./Newsday; 17, 19: New York Daily News Photo; 20, 23, 25: Brad Watson/Calgary Flames; 26, 29, 31, 47, 49, 89, 98, 101, 104, 113, 115: Wide World Photos; 61: Texas Rangers Baseball Club; 62, 67: Nancy Crampton; 65, 77: AP/Wide World Photos; 80, 85: London Pictures Service/Lord Snowdon; 83: British Information Services; 92, 95, 97: © National Geographic Society/Hugo Von Lawick; 107, 109: Pan American World Airways; 121: Bettina Cirone.

World of Vocabulary, Orange Level, Third Edition
Sidney J. Rauch   Zacharie J. Clements

ISBN 1-55675-364-0

Printed in the United States of America
10 9 8 7 6

SIDNEY J. RAUCH is Professor of Reading and Education at Hofstra University, and senior author of the World of Vocabulary series. He has been a visiting professor at numerous universities and is active as a lecturer and consultant. As a member of the College Proficiency Examination Committee of the New York State Education Department, he was involved in the certification of reading personnel. He has given in-service courses and has served as consultant to over thirty school districts in New York, Florida, North Carolina, South Carolina, and the U.S. Virgin Islands. Dr. Rauch was named Reading Educator of the Year for 1985 by the New York State Reading Association.

As coauthor and editor, his texts include: A Need to Read series, *Handbook for the Volunteer Tutor (Second Edition), Guiding the Reading Program, Cloze Thinking, Mastering Reading Skills,* and *Corrective Reading in the High School Classroom.* He is author of the Barnaby Brown books, a children's series. Dr. Rauch's many articles have appeared in *The Reading Teacher, Journal of Reading, Reading World,* and conference proceedings of the International Reading Association.

ZACHARIE J. CLEMENTS is president of the Corporation for Motivation in Education and Enterprise and one of the most sought after speakers in North America. He was formerly Professor of Education at the University of Vermont. He has taught in public schools from grade 6 through high school. Dr. Clements has developed and implemented training programs in the teaching of corrective reading and reading in secondary school content areas. He has conducted numerous teacher training institutes for the local, state, and national governments and has served as a consultant and lecturer to school districts throughout the United States and Canada. Dr. Clements has authored or coauthored *Sense and Humanity in Our Schools, Resource Kit for Teaching Basic Literacy in the Content Area, Units for Dynamic Teaching Program,* and *Profiles: A Collection of Short Biographies.*

CONTENTS 〰〰〰〰〰〰〰〰〰〰〰〰〰

PHILIPPE PETIT THE ROPE DANCER

In 1974, most Americans had never heard of Philippe Petit, a French aerialist. On August 7 of that year, they were startled to see Petit stroll casually across a wire 1,350 feet above the New York City skyline . As usual, he did not use a net. He had sneaked into the World Trade Center at night and set up his wires. It was an exciting day for pedestrians , but just a typical sky walk for Mr. Petit.

His wire-walking career began in France when he performed between the two towers of the cathedral of Notre Dame in Paris in 1971. He brought back a tradition from the Middle Ages, when jugglers and acrobats entertained audiences at the cathedral. People watched Petit in amazement . One writer said, "Petit does all that can be done on a tightrope but fall asleep."

Since 1974, Petit has used his wire to cross between two wings of a French palace, a 294-foot valley in Switzerland, Grand Central Station in New York City, and the area between the Arab and Jewish sections of Jerusalem. He tried to perform with a circus, for a while, but he found the work unsatisfactory. The circus' setup led to Petit's only fall. Since then, he has used only his own wires.

Petit dislikes the word daredevil . He is not trying to frighten people. He is expressing himself in a personal art form. He insists he is putting on not the world's most dangerous performance , but "beautiful and fantastic shows."

~~~~~~~~~~~~~~~~~ UNDERSTANDING THE STORY ~~~~~~~~~~~~~~~~~

▶ Circle the letter next to each correct statement.

1. Another good title for this story might be:
   a. "Walking the Wire"
   b. "From France to New York"
   c. "An Old Tradition"

2. Petit left the circus because
   a. he was not paid enough money.
   b. he could not perform as he liked.
   c. he did not like being called a daredevil.

▶Here are the ten vocabulary words in this lesson. Write them in alphabetical order in the blank spaces below.

stroll	casually	skyline	pedestrians	typical
cathedral	amazement	daredevil	personal	performance

1. _____

2. _____

3. _____

4. _____

5. _____

6. _____

7. _____

8. _____

9. _____

10. _____

WHAT DO THE WORDS MEAN?

▶Here are some meanings of the ten vocabulary words in this lesson. Four words have been written beside their meanings. Write the other six words next to their meanings.

1. _____skyline_____ outline of buildings against the sky

2. _____ a large church

3. _____ people who walk

4. _____ average or ordinary

5. _____ a person who performs with great risks

6. _____strolled_____ walked in a leisurely way

7. _____ in a relaxed or comfortable manner

8. _____personal_____ private; special to one person

9. _____amazement_____ great surprise

10. _____ the giving of some kind of show

4

▶Use the vocabulary words in this lesson to complete the following sentences. Use each word only once. The first one has been done for you.

stroll	casually	skyline	pedestrians	typical
cathedral	amazement	daredevil	personal	performance

1. Philippe Petit has surprised many _____pedestrians_____ on their way to work.

2. They look up in _____ to see him performing high over their heads.

3. In his _____ , Petit may dance, lie down, and even kneel.

4. He performs _____ , as if his act were natural.

5. He often performs at a _____ because the twin stone towers make a natural support for his wires.

6. For a _____ performance, Petit may have to spend hours or even days setting up his wires.

7. He likes being part of the _____ of a great city.

8. Petit is not a _____ because he is not trying to risk his life.

9. On the other hand, would you like to _____ across a wire hundreds of feet in the air?

10. The high wire is a _____ art form to Petit who often participates in shows which include stories and music.

▶Look at the picture. What words come into your mind other than the ones you just matched with their meanings? Write them on the blank lines below. To help you get started, here are two good words:

1. _____daring_____
2. _____frightening_____
3. _____
4. _____
5. _____
6. _____
7. _____
8. _____
9. _____
10. _____

▶Each nonsense word contains all the letters in one of the vocabulary words for this lesson. Can you unscramble them? Write your answers in the blanks on the right. The first one has been done for you.

Nonsense Words	Vocabulary Words	Nonsense Words	Vocabulary Words
1. desperitans	pedestrians	6. mefacnorerp	
2. laiddveer		7. zetamamne	
3. pylacit		8. lyaulcas	
4. roaplesn		9. lortsl	
5. lyksien		10. tradcheal	

~~~~~~~~~~~~~~ COMPLETE THE STORY ~~~~~~~~~~~~~~

▶Here are the ten vocabulary words for this lesson:

stroll	casually	skyline	pedestrians	typical
cathedral	amazement	daredevil	personal	performance

▶Four vocabulary words have already been used in this story. They are underlined. There are six blank spaces in the story. Use the other six vocabulary words to fill in the blank spaces.

Philippe Petit gave his first _____ on a rope between two trees in his parents' back yard. To the _____ of his friends, he could juggle, sing, or dance on the wire. Petit likes to perform for passing pedestrians on the streets of New York. He will _____ easily between two trees or between the towers of a great cathedral. People in Paris and New York have grown used to this man on their _____.

Petit sees his work as a personal art form. He does not like to be called a _____. He sees himself as a _____ artist who happens to work high above the streets. He may see his career casually, but astonished onlookers do not!

6

Learn More About Aerialists

▶Do the three exercises below on a separate sheet of paper or in your notebook. Then turn them in to your teacher.

1 There have been other famous aerialists and daredevils. Ask your teacher or librarian for help in learning about one of these men: Harry Houdini, Charles Blondin, Jules Leotard, Steven McPeak. Report your findings to your class.

2 Imagine that you are performing one of Philippe Petit's aerial tricks. How would you feel as you prepared to step on to the wire hundreds of feet above the ground? What makes you perform these stunts? Write a paragraph describing the feelings of the aerialist performing on the high wire.

3 Where would you like to see Petit perform? Is there a building or a natural site near your home where he could put on his act? Think carefully about what Petit requires to be able to perform. Then write a letter to Petit and suggest he perform at the site you have chosen. Be sure to give reasons that support your choice.

⊁ 2 ONSCREEN AND OFFSCREEN PARENT

Most television ⎡viewers⎤ recognize Phylicia Rashad as Clair Hux-table, Bill Cosby's onscreen wife on *The Cosby Show*. The Huxtables raise five television children, and the ⎡cast⎤ now seems like an ⎡average⎤ American family.

It gets a little more ⎡complicated⎤ off screen. Phylicia is married to Ahmad Rashad, the former Minnesota Vikings wide receiver. They have a baby girl named Condola. In addition, Phylicia has a son by a ⎡former⎤ marriage and Ahmad has three children from his former marriage. Still, everyone seems to get along cheerfully.

Phylicia is up every morning making breakfast. "We're talking eggs and grits, not cheese danish," she says. Then it's off to the ⎡studio⎤ to film another ⎡segment⎤ of *Cosby*. Baby Condola goes, too, and plays happily in a room filled with toys from Bill Cosby. On the set, the other cast members treat Condola like the littlest member of the TV family.

How does she feel about ⎡balancing⎤ a career and a large fam-ily? She likes it. "All the women in my family are doers," she explains. Her quiet pride is ⎡obvious⎤ as she talks about her ⎡extended⎤ family. And she brings some of this experience to *The Cosby Show*. "Bill told me I got the part by being a mom. He said I did the scenes about homework with a knowing look in my eye."

~~~~~~~~~~~~~~~~ UNDERSTANDING THE STORY ~~~~~~~~~~~~~~~~

▶ **Circle the letter next to each correct statement.**

1. The main idea of this story is:
   a. Phylicia Rashad is a talented actress.
   b. Phylicia Rashad likes children.
   c. Phylicia Rashad has a busy and interesting life.

2. You can tell that Bill Cosby likes Condola Rashad because
   a. he lets her come to the studio.
   b. he fills her room with toys.
   c. he chose her mother for his show.

9

▶ Here are the ten vocabulary words in this lesson. Write them in alphabetical order in the blank spaces below.

viewers	cast	average	complicated	former
studio	segment	balancing	obvious	extended

1._____   6._____

2._____   7._____

3._____   8._____

4._____   9._____

5._____   10._____

~~~~~~~~~~~~ WHAT DO THE WORDS MEAN? ~~~~~~~~~~~~

▶ Here are some meanings of the ten vocabulary words in this lesson. Four words have been written beside their meanings. Write the other six words next to their meanings.

1._____ easy to see

2._____extended_____ larger than usual

3._____ actors in a play

4._____ difficult; tangled

5._____balancing_____ keeping things equal

6._____ one episode of a television show

7._____studio_____ place where a television show is acted

8._____ earlier

9._____viewers_____ people who watch television

10._____ typical; usual

10

▶ Use the vocabulary words in this lesson to complete the following sentences. Use each word only once. The first one has been done for you.

viewers	cast	average	complicated	former
studio	segment	balancing	obvious	extended

1. Phylicia Rashad is _____balancing_____ a family and her career.

2. Her _____ family includes a child of her own and three of her husband's, as well as a new baby.

3. Her life is _____ by having to work and be a mother and a wife.

4. Her husband is a _____ wide receiver for the Minnesota Vikings.

5. Other members of the _____ enjoy working with Phylicia on *The Cosby Show.*

6. The program seems to be the story of an _____ American family.

7. It is _____ that much of the show's success is due to Bill Cosby.

8. He seems to be able to draw _____ of the program into the story of the Huxtable family.

9. Each _____ of the program has humor, love, and a lesson.

10. Phylicia Rashad enjoys going to the _____ with her baby to film each episode.

~~~~~~~~~~~~~ USE YOUR OWN WORDS ~~~~~~~~~~~~~

▶ Look at the picture. What words come into your mind other than the ones you just matched with their meanings? Write them on the blank lines below. To help you get started, here are two good words:

1. _____award_____
2. _____proud_____
3. _____
4. _____
5. _____
6. _____
7. _____
8. _____
9. _____
10. _____

DO THE CROSSWORD PUZZLE

▶In the crossword puzzle, there is a group of boxes, some with numbers in them. There are also two columns of definitions, one for "across" and the other for "down." **Do the puzzle. Each of the words in the puzzle will be one of the vocabulary words in this lesson. There is one vocabulary word you will not use.**

Across

3. easily seen
5. ordinary; typical
7. difficult
8. people who watch a show

Down

1. keeping things equal
2. earlier
4. one episode
6. beyond or more than
7. actors in a play or show

COMPLETE THE STORY

▶Here are the ten vocabulary words for this lesson:

viewers	cast	average	complicated	former
studio	segment	balancing	obvious	extended

▶There are six blank spaces in the story. Four vocabulary words have already been used in this story. They are underlined. Use the other six words to fill in the blank spaces.

It can be very _____ to put on a television show. First of all you have to hire the _____ , or actors who will put on your show. Then you have to find a studio where you can build sets and rehearse your show. The show might be practiced in a _____ barn or even in a basement. Rehearsal time is short and it is rarely extended by even a day.

Suppose your show is only one _____ of a regular program. The average program may have two or three different directors. You will find yourself _____ your ideas with the ideas of the other directors. It cannot be _____ to viewers that there are different directors.

12

Learn More About Television

▶Do the three exercises below on a separate sheet of paper or in your notebook. Then turn them in to your teacher.

1 Shows about families are always popular. Choose another program about a family. Write a paragraph telling why you like the show. If you do not like programs about families, choose any show you enjoy watching on television.

2 The Emmy Awards are presented every year to honor the best shows and performances on television that season. Use a *World Almanac* to find the answers to these questions:

1. Who won the Emmy last year for Best Actor?
2. Who won the Emmy last year for Best Actress?
3. Which program was chosen for Best Comedy Series?
4. Who won the Emmy for Best Actress in a Comedy Series?
5. Who was the Best Supporting Actor in a Comedy Series?

See if you can learn if these winners have won any other awards.

3 Bill Cosby has been a very successful television actor. See if you can find out what else he has done. You may use magazines, biographical dictionaries, and other reference sources to learn about his career. Write a paragraph or two describing Cosby's career.

Don't be surprised if you are on an excursion and you see a giant waterfowl next to the road. There has been a giant duck on Long Island, New York, for more than fifty years. It is not a real bird, but a rugged structure made of wire, cement, and a plaster-like material called stucco . Often called Big Duck, it was built in 1931.

There used to be a store inside this huge bird, but it has been empty for many years. Although the duck is large enough to be seen by passing aircraft , the store was small. It sold produce from a local farm.

When the land around the duck was sold, people feared that the amazing bird would be torn down. Local officials then decided the duck must not be abandoned . It was moved to a new location.

The duck's migration was treacherous . The bulky bird was placed on a flatbed truck. This was not easy, since the duck weighs ten tons. However, it was safely moved to a park. There, people can admire its bright orange bill and white "feathers." Later the same year, friends of the duck relit the duck's eyes. The "eyes" were taillights from a Model T Ford.

At some point, Big Duck will roost in a museum park with a classic 1950s diner and a farm stand shaped like a witch's hat. In its present home, the duck has received a great deal of attention. A landscaper has even planted flowers around it. As always, people drive by and "quack" a smile.

∿∿∿∿∿∿∿∿∿ UNDERSTANDING THE STORY ∿∿∿∿∿∿∿∿∿

▶ **Circle the letter next to each correct statement.**

1. Another good title for this story might be:
   a. "The Dangers of Moving"
   b. "How to Build a Bird"
   c. "An Unusual Landmark"

2. The sentence, "Local officials then decided the duck must not be abandoned" means that
   a. government people would not let the duck be destroyed.
   b. local politicians were fighting over the duck.
   c. people from the area were unsure what to do about the duck.

▶ Here are the ten vocabulary words in this lesson. Write them in alphabetical order in the blank spaces below.

excursion	rugged	stucco	aircraft	bulky
produce	abandoned	migration	treacherous	waterfowl

1. _____   6. _____

2. _____   7. _____

3. _____   8. _____

4. _____   9. _____

5. _____   10. _____

~~~~~~~~~~~ WHAT DO THE WORDS MEAN? ~~~~~~~~~~~

▶ Here are some meanings of the ten vocabulary words in this lesson. Two words have been written beside their meanings. Write the other eight words next to their meanings.

1. _____treacherous_____ very dangerous

2. _____ deserted; left behind

3. _____ any machine that flies

4. _____ a plaster-like material used in building

5. _____ trip taken for interest or pleasure; a short journey

6. _____ tough, strong

7. _____migration_____ the act of moving from one place to another

8. _____ fruit or vegetables

9. _____ any swimming bird

10. _____ large and heavy

▶Use the vocabulary words in this lesson to complete the following sentences. Use each word only once. The first one has been done for you.

aircraft	migration	abandoned	rugged	bulky
excursion	treacherous	produce	stucco	waterfowl

1. Even from an _____aircraft_____ , you could see the huge duck on the ground.

2. Moving a building can be _____.

3. We went on our _____ through the country last Tuesday.

4. Our house has walls made of_____.

5. Our little dog felt_____ when we were out all day Tuesday.

6. On our way home, we stopped off to buy some_____for that night's dinner.

7. Our house is very_____, and it was not damaged by last night's hurricane.

8. The_____ of the birds was amazing because they traveled over 2,000 miles.

9. The furniture was hard to move because it was_____.

10. A duck is a type of_____.

▶Look at the picture. What words come into your mind other than the ones you just matched with their meanings? Write them on the blank lines below. To help you get started, here are two good words:

1. _____gigantic_____
2. _____amusing_____
3. _____
4. _____
5. _____
6. _____
7. _____
8. _____
9. _____
10. _____

▶ The story you read has many interesting words that were not underlined as vocabulary words. Six of these words are listed below. Can you think of a synonym for each of these words? Remember, a **synonym** is a word that means the same or nearly the same as another word. *Tear* and *rip* are synonyms. **Write the synonym in the blank space next to the word.**

1. surprised _____

2. giant _____

3. structure _____

4. material _____

5. location _____

6. bill _____

COMPLETE THE STORY

▶ Here are the ten vocabulary words for this lesson:

stucco	produce	excursion	aircraft	bulky
rugged	abandoned	treacherous	migration	waterfowl

▶ There are eight blank spaces in the story below. Two vocabulary words have already been used in the story. They are underlined. Use the other six words to fill in the blank spaces.

Joan and her family lived on a farm. They were rugged people who worked the land. Some days, they spent hours lifting _____ bales of hay. The _____ they grew was sold. It was harvest time, and Joan felt that if she went on an excursion for even a few hours, her family might feel she had _____ them. She wasn't sure what to do.

Joan had a chance to fly in a small _____. Her mother might think this was a _____ activity, but Joan knew that the pilot was good. Joan's parents gave permission. Soon she was high in the air watching her family's tiny _____ house from above. The most thrilling sight of all was seeing the _____ of a band of _____ from the air.

18

Learn More About Architecture

▶Do the three exercises below on a separate sheet of paper or in your notebook. Then turn them in to your teacher.

1   The big duck in the story is actually an example of a special kind of architecture. Ask your teacher or librarian to help you find out more about buildings made in the form of animals or everyday objects. What are some examples of this kind of architecture? Why and how were they built?

2   You can make a small sculpture that is similar to the duck in the story. Find out how to make it out of papier-mâché or plaster of Paris. Write out a plan stating what kind of sculpture you want to make and exactly how you will do it. If possible, ask your parents if you can make the sculpture at home.

3   When a structure is designated as a landmark, it is illegal to knock it down or drastically change it. Ask your teacher or librarian to help you find out how a building gets landmark status in your community. Write an explanation of the procedure.

Sergei Priakin (SAYR-gay pree-AHK-un) plays right wing on his hockey team. Since 1983, he has scored only 4 goals and 11 assists. What makes this 6-foot 3-inch, 210-pound hockey player so interesting? He is the first Soviet athlete to play for a North American team. He was hired by the Canadian Calgary Flames in 1989. They expect a hot future for their newest Flame.

"I'll guarantee you he'll get 20 goals in this league ," says one league coach. The coach explained that Soviet hockey players train harder than many North Americans. He expects Priakin to play well against American teams.

Priakin gave an opinion of North American players. "I thought the game would be more physical than it was," he said of his first game. "I expected the game would be somewhat faster."

Priakin's total salary is more than $500,000 a year, but he will see only part of that. Most of the money will go to a Soviet hockey league. Priakin will get an allowance and money for clothes. This seems to satisfy Priakin. He says he just wants to play hockey.

There are some problems for Priakin. Other players resent his high salary. One player said, "I know it is a touchy thing to say, but I don't think it's a good idea to have the Soviets play over here. He's taking a job from North Americans. I don't like it."

But Priakin is happy to be in Canada. "The rink is packed with people," he says. "It is great to play under conditions like that." Other Soviet players are sure to follow Priakin. The Cold War may thaw on the ice of a hockey rink!

UNDERSTANDING THE STORY

▶ **Circle the letter next to each correct statement.**

1. Another good title for this story might be:
   a. "How Hockey is Played"
   b. "A New Kind of Hockey Player"
   c. "Canadian Sports"

2. From this story, you can conclude that
   a. hockey players earn a lot of money.
   b. Soviet hockey is exciting.
   c. people are interested in Sergei Priakin.

▶ Here are the ten vocabulary words in this lesson. Write them in alphabetical order in the blank spaces below.

athlete	guarantee	league	opinion	physical
salary	allowance	satisfy	resent	thaw

1. _____

2. _____

3. _____

4. _____

5. _____

6. _____

7. _____

8. _____

9. _____

10. _____

~~~~~~~~~~ WHAT DO THE WORDS MEAN? ~~~~~~~~~~

▶ Here are some meanings of the ten vocabulary words in this lesson. Four words have been written beside their meanings. Write the other six words next to their meanings.

1. _____ weekly or monthly spending money

2. _____physical_____ using the body

3. _____ promise; be sure of

4. _____athlete_____ someone who plays a sport well

5. _____opinion_____ belief or understanding

6. _____ union; group; association

7. _____ to please or make happy

8. _____ money paid for work or a job

9. _____ dislike; feel annoyed by

10. _____thaw_____ melt

22

▶Use the vocabulary words in this lesson to complete the following sentences. Use each word only once. The first one has been done for you.

athlete	guarantee	league	opinion	physical
salary	allowance	satisfy	resent	thaw

1. An _____athlete_____ may play several sports well.

2. Playing hockey well seems to _____ Priakin.

3. Priakin played for a hockey _____ in the Soviet Union.

4. The Flames _____ that Priakin will do well in Canada.

5. Hockey is a _____ game using energy and skill.

6. One league coach has a very high _____ of Priakin as a hockey player.

7. Most of Priakin's _____ will go to the Soviet Union.

8. Priakin must pay for food and rent out of his _____.

9. American hockey players may _____ the money paid to Sergei Priakin.

10. The ice in a rink may _____ if special machinery does not keep it frozen.

▶Look at the picture. What words come into your mind other than the ten vocabulary words used in this lesson? Write these words on the blank lines below. To help you get started, here are two good words:

1. _____fast_____
2. _____uniform_____
3. _____
4. _____
5. _____
6. _____
7. _____
8. _____
9. _____
10. _____

▶ In each of the following lists of words, one word does not belong. Circle that word. You may use a dictionary.

1.	resent	dislike	encourage	hate	begrudge
2.	promise	predict	guarantee	lie	pledge
3.	perform	please	complete	satisfy	anger
4.	independent	league	union	alliance	club
5.	salary	debt	wages	earnings	allowance

═══════ COMPLETE THE STORY ═══════

▶ Here are the ten vocabulary words for this lesson:

athlete	guarantee	league	opinion	physical
salary	allowance	satisfy	resent	thaw

▶ There are six blank spaces in the story. Four vocabulary words have already been used in this story. They are underlined. Use the other six words to fill in the blank spaces.

What makes a good hockey player? Each of us has a strong

_____ about this question. Each player must be a

good all-round athlete. Hockey players must be able to take the

_____ demands of the sport. Of course, players

expect to practice many hours every day. Players do not

_____ this constant practice. They know it works!

Still, there is no guarantee that a player will play in every game. Only

the best players see action every time.

    The average hockey player does not earn a high

_____ . Yet, money does not seem to be a hockey

player's goal. Just playing the game seems to satisfy most hockey

players. Hockey players learn to live on an _____ so

they can pay for their food and clothing. Soon, other Soviet players

may be hired by North American teams. A_____ in

the Cold War does not worry most players. There is plenty of room

for good players in any league.

Learn More About Athletes

▶Do the three exercises below on a separate sheet of paper or in your notebook. Then turn them in to your teacher.

1 You can see from the story that some Americans resent players from other countries. How do you feel about foreign athletes? Imagine that you are writing a letter to the editor of a sports paper. In your letter, tell the editor how you feel about players from other countries. Explain why you think these players are good or bad for American sports.

2 Make a list of athletes from other countries who play for North American sports teams. (You may use an almanac or other reference source.) Describe each player in a short paragraph. Tell where the player was born. Include the team and sport the athlete plays. If you can find pictures of the athletes, attach the photographs to your paragraphs.

3 Soviet players must give much of their salary to their Soviet sports leagues. Write a paragraph explaining why this custom seems fair or unfair to you. It might help you to know that Soviet athletes are given free housing, food, and training while they develop their skills.

5 LONDON'S HISTORIC TOWER

London, England, is a city of history and tradition . Every year thousands of visitors flock to this busy capital. They visit places like Buckingham Palace, and the Tower of London.

The Tower is actually a castle covering about eighteen acres. It is the oldest and most historic building in London. It was built almost 900 years ago!

The Tower of London has played an important role in English history. It was first used as a fortress. In later years, the Tower served as a palace for several kings.

For many centuries, part of the Tower was used as a prison. When a prisoner was sent to the Tower, he or she was rarely heard from again. Many people suffered terrible tortures there. Some were even beheaded .

Today, the Tower is a tourist attraction . The fabulous crown jewels are housed here. This is a famous collection of diamonds and other valuable gems. Another worthwhile display is the national collection of armor. There is an exhibit of ancient weapons and firearms. The tourist can even see the fiendish tor- ture devices that were used long ago in the Tower.

Many people feel that a trip to England wouldn't be complete without a visit to the historic Tower of London.

〰〰〰〰〰〰〰〰 UNDERSTANDING THE STORY 〰〰〰〰〰〰〰

▶Circle the letter next to each correct statement.

1. The sentence that best expresses the main idea of this story is:
   a. The most violent torture devices were used in the Tower of London.
   b. The Tower of London is the center of England's history.
   c. The Tower of London is a tourist attraction well worth visiting.

2. Even though it doesn't say so in the story, you get the idea that
   a. London is becoming overcrowded with tourists.
   b. the British people liked to remember their past history.
   c. the Tower will soon have to be rebuilt because of old age.

▶ Here are the ten vocabulary words in this lesson. Write them in alphabetical order in the blank spaces below.

fiendish	devices	role	collection	fabulous
tradition	flock	worthwhile	attraction	beheaded

1. _____   6. _____

2. _____   7. _____

3. _____   8. _____

4. _____   9. _____

5. _____   10. _____

▶ Here are some meanings of the ten vocabulary words in this lesson. Four words have been written beside their meanings. Write the other six words next to their meanings.

1. _____ beliefs and customs handed down from generation to generation

2. _____flock_____ gather together

3. _____ part played in life

4. _____ chopped off the head of

5. _____attraction_____ something very popular which people enjoy visiting

6. _____ astonishing

7. _____collection_____ a group of different things gathered together

8. _____ having real merit

9. _____ devilish; very cruel

10. _____devices_____ mechanical apparatuses or machines for special purposes

28

▶ Use the vocabulary words in this lesson to complete the following sentences. Use each word only once. The first one has been done for you.

fabulous	tradition	attraction	role	flock
beheaded	fiendish	collection	worthwhile	devices

1. It is difficult to name the biggest tourist ___attraction___ , but the Tower of London is near the top.

2. The history of England includes some famous stories about the _____ of the Tower of London.

3. It is a _____ for guards at the Tower to wear a special uniform.

4. People _____ around these guards and ask them to pose for photographs.

5. Kings overthrown and sent to the Tower were often _____.

6. The Tower contains a famous _____ of arms and armor.

7. When you visit the Tower, you can see _____ used to torture prisoners.

8. The instruments of torture can only be described as _____.

9. No matter how busy you are it would be _____ to visit the Tower.

10. Very few treasures are so carefully guarded as the _____ crown jewels of England.

▶ Look at the picture. What words come into your mind other than the ones you just matched with their meanings? Write them on the blank lines below. To help you get started, here are two good words:

1. _____soldiers_____
2. _____erect_____
3. _____
4. _____
5. _____
6. _____
7. _____
8. _____
9. _____
10. _____

▶In a crossword puzzle, there is a group of boxes, some with numbers in them. There are also two columns of words or definitions, one for "across" and the other for "down." **Do the puzzle. Each of the words in the puzzle will be one of the vocabulary words in this lesson.**

Across

2. gather together

4. a group of different things

5. beliefs and customs

6. machines

Down

1. having merit

3. part played in life

▶Here are the ten vocabulary words for this lesson:

fiendish	devices	role	collection	fabulous
tradition	flock	worthwhile	attraction	beheaded

▶**There are six blank spaces in the story below. Four vocabulary words have already been used in the story. They are underlined. Use the other six words to fill in the blank spaces.**

There is a castle deep in the forests of Germany that has played a big

_____ in the development of many horror stories.

Tradition has it that vampires once lived in the castle. One legend

says that a prince was _____ in the castle's dungeon.

Today, however, it is a popular attraction to which thousands of

visitors _____ every year. The castle is located on the

top of a mountain and has a fabulous view of a deep valley. Inside the

castle is a museum with a _____ of torture

_____ . Many visitors are sure these machines were

designed by a _____ mind. A trip to the castle would

be a worthwhile visit.

30

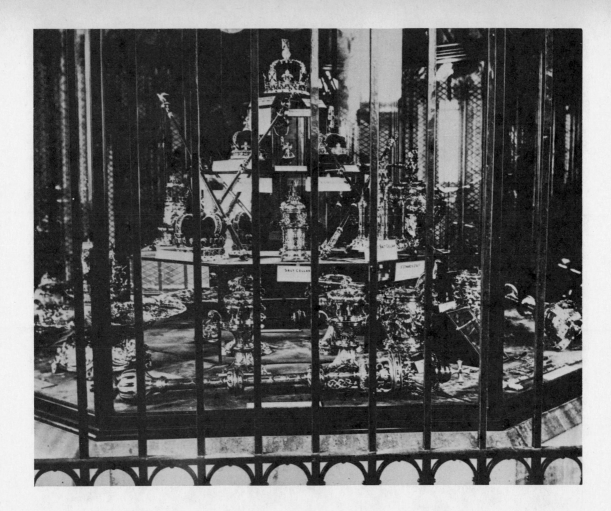

Learn More About England

▶ **Do the three exercises below on a separate sheet of paper or in your notebook. Then turn them in to your teacher.**

1 Do some research on London in your school library. Then make a list of five tourist attractions in the city, besides the Tower of London.

2 Richard II held many prisoners in the Tower of London. Ask your teacher or librarian to help you find out about this man. Write a short paragraph describing him.

3 What are the crown jewels of England? Write several sentences describing them.

THE "CIVILIZED" CHIMP

Washoe is a young female chimpanzee . She is no ordinary chimp, though. Scientists are conducting a research project with her. They want to see how civilized she can become. Already she does many things a human being can do.

For example, she has been learning how to indicate her needs to people. The scientists are teaching her sign language. When she wants to be picked up, Washoe points up with one finger. She rubs her teeth with her finger when she wants to brush her teeth. She does this after every meal.

Washoe has also been trained to think out and solve problems. Once she was put in a room with food hanging from the ceiling . It was too high to reach. After she surveyed the problem, she got a tall box to stand on. The food was still too high to be reached. Washoe found a long pole. Then she stood on the box, grasped the pole, and knocked down the food with the pole.

Washoe lives like a human, too. The scientists keep her in a fully furnished house trailer. After a hard day in the laboratory , she goes home. There she plays with her toys. She even enjoys watching television before going to bed.

Scientists hope to learn more about people by studying our closest relative in the primate group—the chimpanzee.

~~~~~~~~~~~~~~~~ UNDERSTANDING THE STORY ~~~~~~~~~~~~~~~~

▶Circle the letter next to each correct statement.

1. The sentence that best expresses the main idea of this story is:
   a. If we could communicate with animals, life would be much simpler.
   b. Scientists should be spending their time on more important things.
   c. The scientific study of animals helps us learn more about ourselves.

2. Even though it doesn't say so in the story, you get the idea that
   a. animals that are studied in laboratories become spoiled and bad tempered.
   b. animals that are raised in laboratories would find life difficult in the jungle.
   c. animals would rather communicate with people than with other animals.

▶Here are the ten vocabulary words in this lesson. Write them in alphabetical order in the blank spaces below.

chimpanzee	primate	furnished	solve	relative
indicate	research	ceiling	laboratory	surveyed

1. _____   6. _____

2. _____   7. _____

3. _____   8. _____

4. _____   9. _____

5. _____   10. _____

▶Here are some meanings of the ten vocabulary words in this lesson. Four words have been written beside their meanings. Write the other six words next to their meanings.

1. _____ place where scientific work is done

2. _____ show; point out

3. _____relative_____ person related to another by blood or marriage

4. _____ investigation; study

5. _____ most intelligent member of the ape family

6. _____primate_____ any of a group of animals regarded as the smartest

7. _____ find the answer; figure out

8. _____ looked over; examined

9. _____ceiling_____ lining on the top side of a room

10. _____furnished_____ supplied with furniture

34

▶ Use the vocabulary words in this lesson to complete the following sentences. Use each word only once. The first one has been done for you.

research	laboratory	surveyed	indicate	ceiling
primate	solve	relative	chimpanzee	furnished

1. The ___chimpanzee___ is considered a highly intelligent animal.

2. One way to check an animal's intelligence is to see how he or she can _____ problems.

3. Another sign of intelligence is the way an animal can _____ things to people.

4. You could almost see the chimp thinking as she _____ the problem.

5. Scientists plan _____ projects to test animals' intelligence.

6. The chimpanzee belongs to a family of animals known as the _____ group.

7. After spending months together in the _____ , the scientist and the chimp seemed to be good friends.

8. To judge by the beautifully _____ trailer, you would have to say that the chimp lives very well.

9. Hanging from the _____ was an old soccer ball to play with.

10. The chimpanzee is smaller than its _____ , the gorilla.

▶ Look at the picture. What words come into your mind other than the ones you just matched with their meanings? Write them on the blank lines below. To help you get started, here are two good words:

1. _____leaf_____
2. _____cup_____
3. _____
4. _____
5. _____
6. _____
7. _____
8. _____
9. _____
10. _____

▶ Look at the vocabulary word *laboratory*. It is made up of ten letters. See how many words you can form by using the letters of this word. Make up at least eight words. Write your words in the spaces below. One has been done for you.

1. _____root_____   6. _____

2. _____   7. _____

3. _____   8. _____

4. _____   9. _____

5. _____   10. _____

~~~~~~~~~~~~~~~ COMPLETE THE STORY ~~~~~~~~~~~~~~~

▶ Here are the ten vocabulary words for this lesson:

indicate	relative	ceiling	surveyed	primate
chimpanzee	laboratory	research	solve	furnished

▶ There are six blank spaces in the story below. Four vocabulary words have already been used in this story. They are underlined. Use the other six words to fill in the blank spaces.

The chimpanzee is a member of the _____ group.
The chimp is a relative of the gorilla, but much smaller. Scientific
_____ has shown that chimps can be taught to
_____ problems. Just like people, chimps have
_____ problems and found solutions. Washoe, for
example, was able to reach some food hanging from the ceiling. In
the _____, chimps have been taught to indicate their
needs to people. Some lucky chimps, like Washoe, even live in
_____ apartments!

Learn More About Apes and Sign Language

▶Do the three exercises below on a separate sheet of paper or in your notebook. Then turn them in to your teacher.

1 Many people think animals are an important tool in scientific research. Others feel using animals in laboratories is cruel and should be against the law. What's your opinion? Think about both sides of the question. Then write a few paragraphs stating and defending your opinion.

2 There are four main members of the ape family. Ask your librarian to help you in naming them. Select one of these animals and write a short paragraph describing the animal you have selected. Be sure to include where they live and how they live in their natural surroundings.

3 Chimps aren't the only primates to use sign language. People use it too! Go to the library and do some research on sign language. Then prepare an oral report about sign language to be given to your class. Show your classmates how to communicate with sign language by actually "sign talking" some words.

She was the most popular actress in America for three years in a row. She made more than 40 movies. Almost singlehandedly, she kept her Hollywood studio from going bankrupt. Incredibly, she was less than ten years old at the time. Shirley Temple was a one-of-a-kind movie star.

Today, Shirley Temple Black lives with her husband near San Francisco, California. Since retiring from films in 1950, she has been U.S. **Ambassador** to Ghana, Chief of **Protocol** for the U.S. State Department, and a member of our United Nations delegation. She also has worked **tirelessly** for many charities. Black **modestly** describes herself as a "former actress."

Black is not always comfortable with her childhood stardom. For a time, she worked in a hospital. One young patient asked her how she could be a little girl every Sunday night on television and an adult on Monday in the hospital. Black said that the Shirley on television was her daughter. Perhaps it is her way of separating her own **identity** from that of the world-famous little girl.

Black is **keenly** proud of her work as a child actress, but she doesn't want to **dwell** in the past. She is an active, busy woman. She recently wrote her **autobiography** , and she told her story in a **straightforward** , unsentimental manner. Black is a lucky woman and she knows it. She has led two full, active, and useful lives. And she really is an **optimist** . The always-cheerful Shirley Temple we see in her films seems to be one part of her movie career that wasn't an act.

~~~~~~~~~~~~~~~~ UNDERSTANDING THE STORY ~~~~~~~~~~~~~~~~

▶ **Circle the letter next to each correct statement.**

1. The main idea of this story is:
   a. Shirley once worked in a hospital.
   b. Shirley has had two rewarding careers.
   c. Shirley lives in San Francisco.

2. From this story, you can also conclude that
   a. Shirley does a good job as ambassador.
   b. Shirley wishes she were still an actress.
   c. Shirley is soon going to star in a new film.

▶Here are the ten vocabulary words in this lesson. Write them in alphabetical order in the blank spaces below.

tirelessly	ambassador	protocol	modestly	identity
keenly	dwell	autobiography	straightforward	optimist

1. _____

2. _____

3. _____

4. _____

5. _____

6. _____

7. _____

8. _____

9. _____

10. _____

▶Here are some meanings of the ten vocabulary words in this lesson. Four words have been written beside their meanings. Write the other six words next to their meanings.

1. _____autobiography_____ life story written by the person who lived it

2. _____ a person who believes things will work out for the best

3. _____ live in; spend time in

4. _____ without resting

5. _____protocol_____ rules of behavior for governments

6. _____ very strongly

7. _____ direct, honest

8. _____modestly_____ humbly

9. _____ambassador_____ government representative to a foreign country

10. _____ sense of self

40

► Use the vocabulary words in this lesson to complete the following sentences. Use each word only once. The first one has been done for you.

tirelessly	ambassador	protocol	modestly	identity
keenly	dwell	autobiography	straightforward	optimist

1. A director of _____protocol_____ makes sure that important government visitors are greeted and cared for properly.

2. Shirley Temple Black does not like to _____ on the past.

3. She wrote her _____ to set the record straight.

4. She talks of her movie career _____ ; she does not boast.

5. Her cheerfulness shows that she is a true _____.

6. As _____ to Ghana, she represented the United States in that country.

7. She feels _____ proud of her career as an actress.

8. She talks about her life in an honest _____ way.

9. She has a strong sense of her own _____ and does not confuse herself with the popular child star that she was.

10. Shirley Temple Black works _____ and with real enthusiasm at any job she undertakes.

► Look at the picture. What words come into your mind other than the ten vocabulary words used in this lesson? Write them on the blank lines below. To help you get started, here are two good words:

1. _____enthusiastic_____
2. _____dancing_____
3. _____
4. _____
5. _____
6. _____
7. _____
8. _____
9. _____
10. _____

▶In a crossword puzzle, there is a group of boxes, some with numbers in them. There are also two columns of words or definitions, one for "Across" and the other for "Down." **Do the puzzle. The words in the puzzle will be vocabulary words in this lesson.**

Down
1. to live or spend time
2. Shirley Temple Black's job in Ghana
4. proper manners for governments
7. "_____ -forward" meaning honest

Across
3. A person who always looks for the best
5. strongly, intensely
6. without resting
8. Temple's life story as she writes it
9. without a boasting or conceited manner

▶Here are the ten vocabulary words for this lesson:

tirelessly	ambassador	protocol	modestly	identity
keenly	dwell	autobiography	straightforward	optimist

▶**There are six blank spaces in the story below. Four vocabulary words have already been used in the story. Use the other six words to fill in the blank spaces.**

Shirley Temple is more than a well-loved movie star. Her identity as a child actress made her famous, but she talks about those years _____ . After all, Black also has been an _____ and supervised _____ for the American government. She is keenly aware of her successes. However, she is unwilling to _____ in the past and relive the glory of any of these activities.

Black worked tirelessly as an actress. She is an optimist and she refuses to be unhappy about the experience. She enjoyed her life as a child star and is not sorry about any of it. In her_____, she tells about the good and bad experiences of her life in a _____ way.

Learn More About Child Stars

▶Do the three exercises below on a separate sheet of paper or in your notebook. Then turn them in to your teacher.

1 Although Shirley Temple is certainly the most famous child star, there are many other children who have been entertainers. Select one of the following actors or actresses and list some interesting facts about his or her life and career: Mickey Rooney, Gary Coleman, Patty Duke, Michael Jackson, Jody Foster, Brooke Shields, or Tempestt Bledsoe. You may find information in an almanac or in periodicals.

2 Imagine that you are Shirley Temple Black. You have been asked what activity in your life makes you proudest. What do you think you would say? Write your speech on a separate sheet of paper. Be ready to explain your answer.

3 Many child actors do not have the normal experiences of childhood. However, they receive praise and support for their work. Write a paragraph explaining whether the lives of child actors are happy. Give reasons to support your opinion.

There are many kinds of schools. High school, business school, and college are just a few examples. Every city and town has at least one of several kinds of schools. But Venice, Florida, can boast of having a very special and unique kind of school. This school is the only one of its kind in the world. Venice, Florida, is the home of Clown College.

Clown College was established by Irvin Feld, president and producer of the Ringling Brothers and Barnum & Bailey Circus. For eight weeks each fall, 50 young people from all over the United States attend Clown College. They are taught everything a clown needs to know.

Some people may think being a clown is easy, but making people laugh is hard work. In Clown College, students learn how to put on makeup . Putting on a humorous face isn't as easy as it looks. Those crazy shoes and costumes are difficult to get used to. The students learn how to develop a funny skit . They learn how to tumble . A carelessly performed flip could result in an accident . All of these subjects take weeks to master.

After graduation the students hope to get a job with "The Greatest Show On Earth." Besides an exciting lifestyle , the circus offers a clown a wonderful opportunity: to bring joy to "children of all ages."

〰〰〰〰〰 UNDERSTANDING THE STORY 〰〰〰〰〰

▶ Circle the letter next to each correct statement.

1. Another good title for this selection might be:
   a. "Getting Ready for the Big Top"
   b. "Schools Without Homework"
   c. "For Children of All Ages"

2. Although it doesn't say so in the selection, you get the idea that
   a. being a clown is the best job in the circus.
   b. clowns are very sad behind that funny makeup.
   c. a number of young people still want to join the circus.

▶ Here are the ten vocabulary words in this lesson. Write them in alphabetical order in the blank spaces below.

college	boast	attend	makeup	humorous
skit	tumble	accident	graduation	lifestyle

1. _____   6. _____

2. _____   7. _____

3. _____   8. _____

4. _____   9. _____

5. _____   10. _____

▶ Here are some meanings of the ten vocabulary words in this lesson. Four words have been written beside their meanings. Write the other six words next to their meanings.

1. _____ advanced school that gives a degree

2. _____ makeup _____ paint applied to the face for a show

3. _____ funny; amusing

4. _____ manner of living

5. _____ skit _____ short act that often contains humor

6. _____ do leaps, springs, somersaults, etc.

7. _____ accident _____ an unexpected injury

8. _____ ceremony for finishing the course of a school or college

9. _____ boast _____ take pride in having; brag

10. _____ go to classes at

46

▶Use the vocabulary words in this lesson to complete the following sentences. Use each word only once. The first one has been done for you.

lifestyle	graduation	skit	accident	tumble
humorous	makeup	college	attend	boast

1. The clown needed at least an hour to get his _____makeup_____ just right.

2. Not many cities can _____ of a school that trains clowns.

3. Venice, Florida, has a unique kind of _____.

4. Some clowns may look sad, but the things they do are very _____.

5. The two clowns were preparing a new _____ for opening day.

6. When you see a clown trip and take a funny _____, remember that it took weeks of practice.

7. To prevent an _____ , students spend hours learning how to fall.

8. Even though 50 people may _____ Clown College, not all will graduate.

9. The exciting _____ of a circus still attracts young people from all over the country.

10. _____ from Clown College can lead to a regular job with Ringling Brothers Circus.

▶Look at the picture. What words come into your mind other than the ones you just matched with their meanings? Write them on the blank lines below. To help you get started, here are two good words:

1. _____flip_____
2. ____spectators____
3. _____
4. _____
5. _____
6. _____
7. _____
8. _____
9. _____
10. _____

▶ In a crossword puzzle, there is a group of boxes, some with numbers in them. There are also two columns of words or definitions, one for "across" and the other for "down". **Do the puzzle. Each of the words in the puzzle will be one of the vocabulary words in this lesson.**

Across

3. paint applied to the face

4. very funny

5. to brag

6. unexpected injury

Down

1. ceremony for finishing a school or college

2. do somersaults

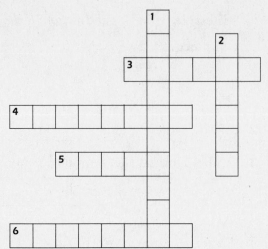

〰〰〰〰〰〰〰〰〰〰〰 COMPLETE THE STORY 〰〰〰〰〰〰〰〰〰〰〰

▶ Here are the ten vocabulary words for this lesson:

college	boast	attend	makeup	humorous
skit	tumble	accident	graduation	lifestyle

▶ **There are six blank spaces in the story below. Four vocabulary words have already been used in the story. They are underlined. Use the other six words to fill in the blank spaces.**

Several weeks had passed since _____ at Clown

College. Now Phyllis, one of the best students at the school, was ready

to begin her first performance at the circus.

Phyllis had arrived early to apply her _____. She

had time to practice her _____. She wanted to do

well—many of her friends planned to _____ this show.

Showtime came and Phyllis began her humorous routine. She could

boast of having learned her lessons well. She could _____

without fear of an accident.

After the performance, Phyllis was happy. She had done very well.

The crowd's applause convinced her that she was going to enjoy her

new _____ with the circus.

48

Learn More About the Circus

▶ Do the three exercises below on a separate sheet of paper or in your notebook. Then turn them in to your teacher.

1 Have you ever been to the circus? Which act did you most enjoy? Write a paragraph about your favorite circus act or performer. Explain why you feel your choice is special.

2 The trapeze artist is one of the most exciting performers in the circus. In your own words describe the kind of man or woman you would have to be to become a great trapeze artist.

3 Write a story starring yourself! In your story, you are a famous lion tamer. You are about to enter a cage filled with ferocious lions and tigers. Several thousand hushed fans are watching. Tell what happens when you enter the cage. Be creative!

9 FLYING MESSENGERS

It was the winter of 1871. The city of Paris, France, was being besieged by the German army. The invaders had severed most lines of communication. How could the people of Paris get news to their friends and relatives outside the city? How could messages be sent back into the city? The Germans would surely intercept them.

The people turned to one of the most ancient means of communication—the homing pigeon. Each message was written on a thin piece of paper. It was inserted into a tube, and clasped onto a pigeon's leg. The pigeons safely carried messages in and out of Paris until the end of the German occupation.

Whether a homing pigeon is taken one mile or 1,200 miles away from its cote, it will always return. The young pigeon is trained to do this. When it's three months old, the pigeon is taken a mile away from home. There, it is set free so it can fly back. A few days later, it is taken three miles from its home and set free again. This mode of training continues until the pigeon is able to return home from long distances.

No one really knows how a homing pigeon can find its way home. Some scientists think these birds navigate by the sun because in bad weather they sometimes get lost. Scientists do know that pigeons can recognize landmarks. Maybe this is what guides them back to their homes.

 UNDERSTANDING THE STORY

▶Circle the letter next to each correct statement.

1. The sentence that best expresses the main idea of this story is:
   a. The winter of 1871 was the worst in French history.
   b. The people of Paris wanted to communicate with their relatives.
   c. Pigeons were among the heroes of the war of 1871.

2. Even though it doesn't say it in the story, you get the idea that
   a. all animals can be trained to find their way home.
   b. the deeds of the pigeons will be retold in many French history books.
   c. pigeons are no longer raised in the city of Paris.

▶Here are the ten vocabulary words in this lesson. Write them in alphabetical order in the blank spaces below.

besieged	cote	intercept	inserted	invaders
navigate	mode	occupation	severed	clasped

1. _____   6. _____

2. _____   7. _____

3. _____   8. _____

4. _____   9. _____

5. _____   10. _____

▀▄▀▄▀▄▀▄▀▄▀ WHAT DO THE WORDS MEAN? ▀▄▀▄▀▄▀▄▀▄

▶Here are some meanings of the ten vocabulary words in this lesson. Four words have been written beside their meanings. Write the other six words next to their meanings.

1. _____ surrounded with armed forces

2. _____invaders_____ attackers; enemies who enter by force

3. _____ cut off

4. _____intercept_____ take or seize on the way from one place to another

5. _____ put into

6. _____clasped_____ fastened tightly

7. _____ possession of a city or country by an enemy

8. _____cote_____ cage or shelter for pigeons

9. _____ method or manner

10. _____ find one's way

52

▶Use the vocabulary words in this lesson to complete the following sentences. Use each word only once. The first one has been done for you.

inserted	mode	navigate	occupation	clasped
severed	cote	besieged	intercept	invaders

1. The _____mode_____ of training used is to start with short distances and build up to the longer distances.

2. In 1871, the French people were _____ by the German army.

3. The _____ of most of France by the enemy separated the people of Paris from the rest of the country.

4. Lines of communication were _____ ; messages could not get out.

5. People thought the Germans would _____ messages sent by land.

6. A trained homing pigeon always returns to its _____.

7. A message can be _____ into a tube and put onto a pigeon's leg.

8. The tube _____ to the pigeon's leg weighed very little.

9. Though the people of Paris were frightened by the _____ , they managed to get messages past them.

10. No one knows exactly how these pigeons _____ long distances, but these birds seem to recognize landmarks.

▶Look at the picture. What words come into your mind other than the ones you just matched with their meanings? Write them on the blank lines below. To help you get started, here are two good words:

1. _____sky_____
2. _____fly_____
3. _____
4. _____
5. _____
6. _____
7. _____
8. _____
9. _____

▶ An *antonym* is a word that means the opposite of another word. *Fast* and *slow* are antonyms. Match the vocabulary words on the left with the antonyms on the right. Write the correct letter in the blank space next to the vocabulary word.

Vocabulary Words

1. _____ inserted

2. _____ invaders

3. _____ clasped

4. _____ severed

Antonyms

a. defenders

b. removed

c. mended

d. released

~~~~~~~~~~~~~~ COMPLETE THE STORY ~~~~~~~~~~~~~~

▶ Here are the ten vocabulary words for this lesson:

besieged	cote	intercept	severed	invaders
navigate	mode	occupation	inserted	clasped

▶ There are six blank spaces in the story below. Four vocabulary words have already been used in this story. They are underlined. Use the other six vocabulary words to fill in the blank spaces.

The Parisians were clever people. When the German army besieged their city, they trained pigeons to be messengers. This was one way they could bridge the severed communication lines. The German _____ would probably try to _____ any other mode of communication. The people _____ a message into a tube. Then they _____ the tube to the pigeon's leg. They had to wait for a sunny day to release the pigeon. They believed pigeons could only _____ by the sun. If it were raining, the pigeon might get lost and not return to its _____ . In this way, the people got news to the outside world until the end of the occupation.

54

Learn More About Communication and the Siege of Paris

▶ Do the three exercises below on a separate sheet of paper or in your notebook. Then turn them in to your teacher.

1 What was the name of the war mentioned in the story in which Paris was besieged? What was the name of the man who was the leader of the German forces? What was his title? What did most people call him?

2 The title of this selection is "Flying Messengers." Can you think of other titles that may work even better? Give it a try. On a sheet of paper, make up at least three titles that could be used for this story.

3 To "communicate" means to make known. How many forms of communication can you list? Describe how you would communicate with your friends by using two of these methods of communication.

10 STRIKEOUT KING

The pitcher taps the ball in his glove. He nods in agreement to the catcher. The crowd tenses . They watch him go into his windup. His arm whips forward. The pitcher hurls the ball toward the plate. At 95 mph, it approaches the plate. The batter swings but misses. It's strike three. The batter is out. The crowd cheers. Nolan Ryan has struck out another batter. He is pleased. It's not an unusual event , though. Nolan Ryan is the strikeout king of base-ball. Ryan has struck out more than 5,000 batters. He's one of the best pitchers in the business.

In 1973, Ryan shattered Sandy Koufax's record for the most strikeouts in a season. Ryan struck out 383 batters. He has had five seasons with more than 300 strikeouts. That's another record. In 1983, Ryan struck out batter number 3,509 of his career. That broke the record. Ryan has kept pitching. He has struck out more batters every season. He holds the record for the most strikeouts of any pitcher ever. It will be a long time before anyone can equal his record.

Ryan has played baseball for more than 20 seasons. He still has one of the best fastballs. In 1974, radar clocked his blazing fastball at 100 mph. Today, he can still throw at 97 mph. He often plays in pain, however. His arm has been injured. Ryan's arm is showing signs of wear and tear. Many fastball pitchers don't last very long. They begin to slow down. Ryan is an outstanding pitcher. He has kept his speed. He is still one of the Texas Rangers' most valuable pitchers. He is still the strikeout king.

UNDERSTANDING THE STORY

▶Circle the letter next to each correct statement.

1. Nolan Ryan is the strikeout king because
   a. he struck out an important player in a World Series.
   b. he plays even though his arm hurts.
   c. he holds so many strikeout records.

2. Nolan Ryan is likely to
   a. keep pitching for another 20 years.
   b. retire from baseball in a few years.
   c. begin pitching a faster fastball.

▶Here are the ten vocabulary words in this lesson. Write them in alphabetical order in the blank spaces below.

agreement	tenses	hurls	approaches	event
shattered	record	blazing	outstanding	equal

1. _____   6. _____

2. _____   7. _____

3. _____   8. _____

4. _____   9. _____

5. _____   10. _____

▶Here are some meanings of the ten vocabulary words in this lesson. Four words have been written beside their meanings. Write the other six words next to their meanings.

1. _____ being of the same opinion

2. _____ becomes nervous or strained

3. _____shattered_____ broke

4. _____ do as well as

5. _____event_____ something that occurs

6. _____ throws hard

7. _____record_____ best that has been done

8. _____ prominent; distinguished

9. _____ unusually fast; like lightning

10. _____approaches_____ comes close to

58

▶ Use the vocabulary words in this lesson to complete the following sentences. Use each word only once. The first one has been done for you.

shattered	tenses	approaches	record	blazing
agreement	hurls	equal	event	outstanding

1. She asked me to be on the team, and I nodded in _____agreement_____ .

2. Very few new players can _____ the power of the really great pitchers.

3. Our team's _____ of twelve wins and no losses was the best in the league.

4. Nolan Ryan has _____ many players' hopes of making a big hit.

5. As the runner _____ home plate, the catcher tries to touch him with the ball.

6. She always _____ up when it's her turn to bat.

7. The shortstop _____ the ball toward first base.

8. The _____ speed of Nolan Ryan's fastball makes it very hard to hit.

9. The game with North High is the big _____ of the season.

10. Most sports writers view Nolan Ryan as an _____ athlete.

▶ Look at the picture. What words come into your mind other than the ten vocabulary words used in this lesson? Write them on the blank lines below. To help you get started, here are two good words:

1. _____power_____
2. _____drive_____
3. _____
4. _____
5. _____
6. _____
7. _____
8. _____
9. _____
10. _____

▶ A **synonym** is a word that means the same or nearly the same as another word. Below are six vocabulary words. They are each followed by four other words or groups of words. One of these words is a synonym; the others are not. **Draw a circle around the word that is a synonym. The first one has been done for you.**

Vocabulary Words   **Synonyms**

1. hurls	hurdles	injures	(throws)	helps
2. shattered	folded	smashed	created	spied
3. remarkable	incredible	talkative	neat	even
4. event	final	long	building	happening
5. approaches	nears	tries	smoothes	trusts
6. blazing	cold	fiery	bloody	dark

~~~~~~~~~~~~~~~ COMPLETE THE STORY ~~~~~~~~~~~~~~~

▶ Here are the ten vocabulary words for this lesson:

shattered	tenses	approaches	record	blazing
agreement	hurls	equal	event	outstanding

▶ There are six blank spaces in the story below. Four vocabulary words already have been used in the story. They are underlined. Use the other six words to fill in the blank spaces.

Nolan Ryan_____ a baseball more than 100 times in a game. Every fastball moves with blazing speed. He also throws a great curve ball. His skill is_____ . How does he do it? There is agreement among sports fans. Ryan has great natural talent. He has an arm that is hard to_____ . There's more to it, though. Ryan approaches pitching like a science. He studies it. He uses his legs and hips, not just his arm. Sometimes Ryan_____ up before a game. But on the mound he's in control. That's how he has_____ so many records. He keeps himself in shape, too.

    Ryan has set many records. He still looks forward to another great event or two. He'd like to play in another World Series. He is sure to add to his strikeout_____ .

Learn More About Baseball

▶ Do the three exercises below on a separate sheet of paper or in your notebook. Then turn them in to your teacher.

1 There are many other great pitchers such as Tom Seaver, Sandy Koufax, Bob Feller, and Walter Johnson. Pick a great pitcher. Do some research on him. Use your school or public library. Then write a few paragraphs about the pitcher's career. Tell why he is considered great.

2 Which baseball team do you like the best? Explain why that team is the team of your choice. Use newspaper stories and sports magazine articles to support your reasons.

3 Pitchers in the American League like Nolan Ryan had an easier time before the "designated hitter rule." This rule went into effect in 1973. Explain what the rule is. (Hint: You can find the answer in a book about baseball.) Then explain how this rule affects the number of strikeouts a pitcher makes.

Toni Morrison, the writer, knows from her past that success requires hard work. During her childhood, her parents fostered good values. Toni grew up in a home where learning was considered important. She graduated from high school with honors. Then she completed four years of college. In 1955, she earned a master's degree in English from Cornell. With this training, she taught English at two colleges. They were Texas Southern and Howard. Later she married and became the mother of two sons. For most people, combining college teaching and marriage would be a full life.

But Toni Morrison has another talent that she can't deny. She is a gifted writer. Her stories about the people she grew up with touch everyone. After many years of research, she wrote *The Bluest Eye*. This was followed by a novel, *Sula*. The reviewers praised her ear for dialogue. They loved her poetic language. Toni Morrison was seen as a keen observer of life in black America. Her most famous book was *Song of Solomon*. It won the National Book Critics Circle Award. This prize gave her worldwide fame. As a result, she is considered one of America's great writers.

These days Toni Morrison is a very active woman. She continues to write, and she is now on the faculty of Princeton University. When she looks back, she credits her parents for their concern about education. Her own career serves as a beacon for other writers to follow.

~~~~~~~~~~~~~~~~ UNDERSTANDING THE STORY ~~~~~~~~~~~~~~~~

▶ Circle the letter next to each correct statement.

1. Another good title for this story might be:
   a. "Why I Became a Writer"
   b. "My Favorite Author"
   c. "The Story of a Successful Writer"

2. Even though it doesn't say it in the story, you can tell that
   a. success depends mainly on good luck.
   b. success is not as important as we think it is.
   c. success is often traced back to the values learned in early childhood.

▶Here are the ten vocabulary words in this lesson. Write them in alphabetical order in the blank spaces below.

research	fostered	dialogue	critics	beacon
deny	honors	active	poetic	gifted

1._____   6._____

2._____   7._____

3._____   8._____

4._____   9._____

5._____   10._____

⠿⠿⠿⠿⠿⠿ WHAT DO THE WORDS MEAN? ⠿⠿⠿⠿⠿⠿

▶Here are some meanings of the ten vocabulary words in this lesson. Four words have been written beside their meanings. Write the other six words next to their meanings.

1._____beacon_____ a guiding light; something or someone to follow

2._____ busy; involved

3._____fostered_____ encouraged; helped make something happen

4._____ conversation between two or more persons

5._____ to say something is untrue; to refuse

6._____ awards

7._____ the study of a topic to find as many facts as possible

8._____poetic_____ referring to language that has the beauty of poetry

9._____critics_____ people who write their opinions of books, plays, movies, music, and painting

10._____ having great ability; talent

64

▶Use the vocabulary words in this lesson to complete the following sentences. Use each word only once. The first one has been done for you.

research	honors	dialogue	critics	beacon
deny	fostered	active	poetic	gifted

1. Toni's parents _____fostered_____ their daughter's wish for education.

2. Toni leads a very _____ life by being a mother, teacher, and author.

3. Writers are very concerned with what the _____ have to say about them.

4. These experts say the way Toni captures the _____ of her characters is outstanding.

5. Only after months of _____ do many writers begin their novels.

6. The National Book Award is but one of the many _____ Toni has won.

7. No one could _____ her skill as a writer.

8. Because her words are so carefully chosen experts call her style _____.

9. Few writers are as _____ as Toni Morrison.

10. Toni's achievements serve as a _____ for other black writers hoping for success.

▶Look at the picture. What words come into your mind other than the ones you have learned in this story? Write them on the blank lines below. To help you get started, here are two good words:

1. _____woman_____
2. _____poet_____
3. _____
4. _____
5. _____
6. _____
7. _____
8. _____
9. _____
10. _____

▶ In each of the following lists of words, one word is out of place. Circle that word. You may use your dictionary.

1.   dialogue   words   language   movement   speech

2.   active   busy   energetic   lively   lazy

3.   honors   awards   defeats   scholarships   grants

4.   denied   prevented   encouraged   stopped   blocked

5.   gifted   able   skilled   awkward   talented

========= COMPLETE THE STORY =========

▶ Here are the ten vocabulary words for this lesson:

beacon	fostered	critics	poetic	gifted
deny	active	honors	dialogue	research

▶ There are six blank spaces in the story below. Four vocabulary words have already been used in this story. They are underlined. Use the other six words to fill in the blank spaces.

Toni Morrison is a woman whose life serves as a beacon for us to do
better. Despite hardships, her parents fostered good values in her.
They taught her to seek education and to be _____
in school. Because she listened, she won many _____
for her school work. Many of her teachers recognized her as a gifted
student.

Today, Toni Morrison is considered one of America's great authors.
Critics praise her writing style. They admire the way she captures the
true _____ of her characters. Her use of language is
so beautiful that other writers call it _____ . Yet, Toni
does not _____ that it takes a lot of effort to write her
stories. Months of _____ are necessary before each
story is finally written.

Learn More About Authors and Writing

▶Do the three exercises below on a separate sheet of paper or in your notebook. Then turn them in to your teacher.

1 Toni Morrison is one of a number of important black authors. Find the names of at least four others and give some titles of what they have written.

2 Try to find out if any authors live in your community. Perhaps you can get your teacher to invite him or her to come to your school to talk to your class.

3 Our story mentions some of the things necessary to become a successful author. They are education, talent, and hard work. Name other qualities necessary to become a successful author.

12 CREATURE OF THE DEEP

You are swimming in the ocean. The sea water is warm and refreshing . Suddenly, a long, snakelike object wraps around your body and pulls you under. You try to struggle free but you can't. Another powerful arm grabs you. There's no hope for escape now. You know you're in the deadly clutch of an octopus !

That's what many people think will happen when a swimmer confronts an octopus. But this unusual creature rarely attacks people. Some octopuses are only as big as your fist. When divers happen by, the average octopus quickly swims away and hides.

The octopus lives in rocky places near shore. It waits in hiding for fish to pass. When a victim swims close enough, the octopus will lash out with one of its eight arms, called tentacles . Then it tears the fish apart with its sharp, parrotlike beak.

In many parts of the world, octopus flesh is a popular food. One way to catch an octopus is to lower jars down to the ocean floor. The jars are left there for several hours. The creatures creep into the jars, which serve as fine hiding places. Then the jars are drawn up to the surface.

Is the octopus an animal to fear? Not really. It is simply another creature doing its best to survive .

﹌﹌﹌﹌ UNDERSTANDING THE STORY ﹌﹌﹌﹌

▶ **Circle the letter next to each correct statement.**

1. The main idea of the story is that
   a. diving near an octopus is dangerous.
   b. catching an octopus is fun.
   c. the octopus is not a creature to fear.

2. Even though it doesn't say it in the story, you can tell that
   a. people often misunderstand the octopus.
   b. the octopus rarely attacks divers.
   c. some people like to eat octopus.

▶Here are the ten vocabulary words in this lesson. Write them in alphabetical order in the blank spaces below.

survive	refreshing	creep	victim	confronts
octopus	tentacles	flesh	clutch	lash

1. _____   6. _____

2. _____   7. _____

3. _____   8. _____

4. _____   9. _____

5. _____   10. _____

▶Here are some meanings of the ten vocabulary words in this lesson. Four words have been written beside their meanings. Write the other six words next to their meanings.

1. _____ makes new again; a pleasing change

2. _____ clutch _____ tight grip or grasp

3. _____ meets face to face; opposes boldly

4. _____ victim _____ person or animal killed, injured, or made to suffer

5. _____ lash _____ strike out at

6. _____ long outgrowths from the main body of an octopus

7. _____ soft substance that covers bones; meat

8. _____ octopus _____ sea animal with a soft body and eight arms

9. _____ crawl; move slowly

10. _____ remain alive; continue to exist

70

▶Use the vocabulary words in this lesson to complete the following sentences. Use each word only once. The first one has been done for you.

refreshing	octopus	victim	flesh	survive
clutch	confronts	tentacles	creep	lash

1. The octopus will often _____lash_____ out at a fish with one of its eight arms.

2. What does an octopus have to do in order to _____ in the world?

3. I had to _____ a nearby rock to avoid getting close to the octopus.

4. Agnes says she gets excited whenever she _____ a new sea creature.

5. With all those arms, the _____ may not be dangerous but it will surely still scare people.

6. A diver will usually only become the _____ of an octopus attack when the octopus is very hungry.

7. Some people say the _____ of an octopus tastes like chicken.

8. An octopus has eight arms, or _____.

9. A swim in the ocean is very _____ after sitting in the hot sun.

10. As the octopus started to _____ toward me, I ran in the opposite direction.

▶Look at the picture. What words come into your mind other than the ones you just matched with their meanings? Write them on the blank lines below. To help you get started, here are two good words:

1. _____water_____
2. _____diver_____
3. _____
4. _____
5. _____
6. _____
7. _____
8. _____
9. _____
10. _____

▶Each nonsense word contains all the letters in one of the vocabulary words for this lesson. Can you unscramble them? Write your answers in the blanks on the right. The first one has been done for you.

Nonsense Words	Vocabulary Words	Nonsense Words	Vocabulary Words
1. firerneghs	refreshing	6. slah	
2. tulcch		7. atnetselc	
3. supotco		8. selfh	
4. rfncostno		9. ecpre	
5. ticvim		10. ruseiv	

▀▀▀▀▀▀▀▀▀▀ COMPLETE THE STORY ▀▀▀▀▀▀▀▀▀▀

▶Here are the ten vocabulary words for this lesson:

survive	refreshing	creep	clutch	confronts
octopus	tentacles	flesh	victim	lash

▶There are six blank spaces in the story. Four vocabulary words have already been used in the story. They are underlined. Use the other six words to fill in the blank spaces.

Another strange sea creature is the squid. It has long, wavy tentacles like the _____ . This creature eats great quantities of fish. When it _____ a possible victim, it will _____ out with one or more of its tentacles and catch it. It is very difficult for any fish to _____ the deadly _____ of a squid. Also like the octopus, small squid will creep into jars lowered to the ocean floor. This makes them easy to catch, which is fortunate because many people enjoy eating squid _____ as part of a refreshing stew.

Learn More About Creatures of the Sea

▶Do the three exercises below on a separate sheet of paper or in your notebook. Then turn them in to your teacher.

1 An octopus is not really a dangerous sea creature, but sharks are. Why are sharks so dangerous? Write a short paragraph telling about these savage creatures of the deep.

2 Make up an episode similar to the one in the first paragraph of the main story. Your adventure doesn't have to be true, but make believe it actually happened to *you!* Let your imagination take over. Be creative!

3 Have you ever visited an aquarium, or would you like to? List five sea creatures you'd particularly like to see. In a short paragraph, tell what it is about each of these creatures that interests you most.

The Chicago Bulls have a basketball marvel . Michael Jordan leads the National Basketball Association in points, steals, and minutes played per game. Largely because of his efforts, the Bulls enjoyed a rally and became the biggest road show in basketball. A member of the Olympic gold medal team in 1984, Jordan is just as special off the court as he is on it.

Jordan grew up in North Carolina. His parents had no special athletic ability . In fact, Jordan himself was cut from his high school basketball team in his sophomore year. That didn't stop him. Jordan entered professional basketball in 1985, and he has practically owned the court ever since.

How does this startling young man respond to the questions about his career? He is surprisingly modest. He cannot even buy groceries without a mob of fans begging for an autograph . Otherwise, he is the same person he was when he played basketball in his backyard in North Carolina.

Jordan is uncomfortable as a superstar, but he is better known that any other living athlete, and he takes this fame seriously. He appears in anti-drug ads because he knows his fame can help the kids who admire him. **Frequently** , Jordan visits hospitals or homes where young fans struggle with serious illnesses. His mother recalls the night he gave a pair of sneakers to a young street kid and fan. Jordan first made the boy promise to go to school the next day, however. And he's sincere ; there were no reporters around at the time. Jordan seems to be a star on the court and off.

wwwwwwwwwwww **UNDERSTANDING THE STORY** wwwwwwwwwwww

▶ **Circle the letter next to each correct statement.**

1. Another good title for this story might be
   a. "A New Basketball Star."
   b. "Michael Jordan's Childhood."
   c. "Being Famous is Fun."

2. Even though it doesn't say so in the story, you can tell that
   a. Michael Jordan is worried about the future.
   b. basketball fans are excited about Michael Jordan.
   c. Michael Jordan wants to live in Chicago.

75

▶Here are the ten vocabulary words in this lesson. Write them in alphabetical order in the blank spaces below.

marvel	rally	ability	practically	startling
autograph	admire	frequently	recalls	sincere

1. _____   6. _____

2. _____   7. _____

3. _____   8. _____

4. _____   9. _____

5. _____   10. _____

▶Here are some meanings of the ten vocabulary words in this lesson. Four words have been written beside their meanings. Write the other six words next to their meanings.

1. _____ often

2. _____ rally _____ new burst of energy

3. _____ signature

4. _____ honest

5. _____ startling _____ surprising

6. _____ almost

7. _____ wonder

8. _____ ability _____ talent

9. _____ remembers

10. _____ admire _____ respect

76

▶ Use the vocabulary words in this lesson to complete the following sentences. Use each word only once. The first one has been done for you.

marvel	rally	ability	practically	startling
autograph	admire	frequently	recalls	sincere

1. No one doubts Michael Jordan's _____ability_____ as an athlete.

2. He is _____ impossible to beat on the basketball court.

3. You see many _____ plays when you watch him.

4. In one _____ , he scored the winning two baskets in the final four seconds of the game.

5. Recently, 50,000 people called for tickets to see this basketball _____ appear on a television talk show.

6. Young fans _____ Jordan and try to be like him.

7. Jordan is _____ recognized and mobbed by fans who want to meet him.

8. He signs his _____ and urges young fans to be good.

9. Michael _____ being dropped from his high school basketball team.

10. In spite of fame, Jordan remains a _____ and modest man.

▶ Look at the picture. What words come into your mind other than the ones you have learned in this story? Write them on the blank lines below. To help you get started, here are two good words:

1. _____powerful_____

2. _____graceful_____

3. _____

4. _____

5. _____

6. _____

7. _____

8. _____

9. _____

10. _____

▶ The **subject** of a sentence names the person, place, or thing that is spoken about. The **predicate** of a sentence is what is said about the subject. For example:

> The young basketball player   scored a shot from midcourt.

▶ *The young basketball player* is the subject the sentence is about. *Scored a shot from midcourt* is the predicate because it tells what the young basketball player did. **In the following sentences draw one line under the subject of the sentence and two lines under the predicate of the sentence.**

1. Many basketball games have attracted large crowds of fans.

2. A good basketball player must be able to dribble, jump, and shoot.

3. The happiest basketball fans are those who see their team win.

4. Jordan leads his team to victory on the court.

5. His concerned coaches are worrying about Jordan's future.

⬩⬩⬩⬩⬩⬩⬩⬩⬩⬩⬩⬩⬩⬩⬩⬩⬩⬩⬩⬩ COMPLETE THE STORY ⬩⬩⬩⬩⬩⬩⬩⬩⬩⬩⬩⬩⬩⬩⬩⬩⬩⬩⬩⬩

▶ **Here are the ten vocabulary words for this lesson:**

marvel	rally	ability	practically	startling
autograph	admire	frequently	recalls	sincere

▶ **There are six blank spaces in the story below. Four vocabulary words have already been used in the story. They are underlined. Use the other six words to fill in the blank spaces.**

Fans admire Jordan's _____ to remain calm under stress. He is a startling player who _____ makes unbelievable shots work. Many think he plays practically alone since his team can hardly keep up with him. Yet his teammates _____ and give him the support he needs.

Off court, Jordan is a sincere young man who always has time to sign an _____ . He _____ his own excitement as a boy when he saw famous players. It is no wonder that so many young people _____ this athletic marvel. They will watch his career with interest in the future.

Learn More About Michael Jordan and Basketball

▶Do the three exercises below on a separate sheet of paper or in your notebook. Then turn them in to your teacher.

1 Try to find some interesting facts about Michael Jordan's career. Look in a sports almanac or other reference book. Make a list of your facts and share them with your classmates.

2 What do you know about the history of basketball? Use the encyclopedia or a sports reference book to find out when and how the game started. Write a paragraph with the facts you have learned.

3 You have many facts about Michael Jordan. What do you think makes Jordan so special? Prepare a speech for your classmates. The title of your speech will be, "Michael Jordan: An Unusual Athlete." In your speech, explain why you think Jordan stands out from other athletes. You may use magazines or other reference sources as you prepare your notes.

DIANA, PRINCESS OF WALES

She's the most photographed person in the world. Her face appears on more magazine covers than that of any leading model. She is Diana, Princess of Wales, wife of the future king of England. From the moment she became **engaged**, she has been in the public eye. She won their hearts quickly. Her beauty and smile are a winning combination. Although Diana comes from a wealthy, **titled** family, she is down-to-earth. She worked as a teacher before she met Prince Charles. The prince made a popular choice.

Being married to a future king is not an easy task. The princess has to attend many public **affairs**. It could be the opening of Parliament or the **dedication** of a hospital. Every eye is on her. The princess must look fresh and **enchanting**. She must be **composed**, no matter how tired she may feel. Diana, Princess of Wales, represents the royal family.

Since the princess was always in the public eye, she had to go from being a shy teenager to being a stylish, self-possessed young woman. She made the change with great success. She has attended public **ceremonies**, waved from the palace **balcony** or the royal **carriage**, and observed other cultures on official trips to foreign countries. She has also proven herself to be a loving mother in her public appearances with her two children, William and Harry.

Public affection for the princess has never lessened. She is still seen as a royal-but-real person.

~~~~~~~~~~~ UNDERSTANDING THE STORY ~~~~~~~~~~~

▶ **Circle the letter next to each correct statement.**

1. Another good title for this story might be:
   a. "The Royal Wedding"
   b. "The Problems of Royalty"
   c. "The Popular Princess"

2. Even though it doesn't say it in the story, you can tell that
   a. the British public is growing tired of royalty.
   b. the princess would probably like a little more privacy.
   c. Prince Charles will soon be king of England.

▶Here are the ten vocabulary words in this lesson. Write them in alphabetical order in the blank spaces below.

affairs	enchanting	carriage	balcony	titled
composed	engaged	observed	ceremonies	dedication

1._____   6._____

2._____   7._____

3._____   8._____

4._____   9._____

5._____   10._____

▶Here are some meanings of the ten vocabulary words in this lesson. Four words have been written beside their meanings. Write the other six words next to their meanings.

1._____dedication_____ the act of opening or naming a public building

2._____ horse-drawn vehicle

3._____ promised to marry

4._____ watched

5._____ member of royalty or nobility

6._____composed_____ calm; showing little emotion

7._____ charming; most attractive

8._____affairs_____ functions; activities

9._____ a kind of porch usually above the ground floor

10._____ceremonies_____ the formalities of a public or private event, such as a coronation or a wedding

82

► Use the vocabulary words in this lesson to complete the following sentences. Use each word only once. The first one has been done for you.

engaged	affairs	carriage	enchanting	titled
observed	ceremonies	dedication	balcony	composed

1. TV pictures of the wedding _____ceremonies_____ were carried to all countries.

2. A princess must be _____ and even-tempered at all times.

3. A palace has more than one _____ where the ruler can wave to subjects.

4. Once Prince Charles and Diana were _____ to be married, reporters followed them everywhere.

5. The princess cut the ribbon at the _____ of the new highway.

6. The princess has a number of _____ ancestors.

7. The crowds were hoping that the royal _____ would stop so they could have a closer look at the princess.

8. A kiss on the balcony was _____ by the crowds below.

9. In describing Diana's beauty many use the word " _____."

10. Attending public _____ is one of the duties of a royal couple.

► Look at the picture. What words come into your mind other than the ones you have learned in this story? Write them on the blank lines below. To help you get started, here are two good words:

1. _____amused_____
2. _____couple_____
3. _____
4. _____
5. _____
6. _____
7. _____
8. _____
9. _____
10. _____

▶ Two of the vocabulary words, *balcony* and *ceremonies,* are nouns. List as many words as you can that describe or tell something about the words *balcony* and *ceremonies*. You can work on this with your classmates. Listed below are some words to help you get started.

balcony	ceremonies
1. _____ upper _____	1. _____ wedding _____
2. _____ decorated _____	2. _____ religious _____
3. _____	3. _____
4. _____	4. _____
5. _____	5. _____
6. _____	6. _____
7. _____	7. _____
8. _____	8. _____
9. _____	9. _____
10. _____	10. _____

▶ Here are the ten vocabulary words for this lesson:

carriage	titled	composed	affairs	engaged
observed	enchanting	ceremonies	dedication	balcony

▶ There are six blank spaces in the story below. Four vocabulary words have already been used in the story. They are underlined. Use the other six words to fill in the blank spaces.

Marrying a future king is not all glamour. It is not easy having everything you do being carefully observed by reporters. When Diana became _____ to Prince Charles, her private life became a thing of the past. She had to appear gracious and composed at public _____, even at the dedication of a factory.

The wedding ceremonies were seen by millions. They were attended by foreign rulers and _____ individuals from many lands. Following the wedding, the young couple climbed into the royal _____ and returned to the palace. To thank the public for their support, they appeared on the palace _____. The princess smiled and looked _____.

Learn More About the Prince and Princess

▶ Do the three exercises below on a separate sheet of paper or in your notebook. Then turn them in to your teacher.

1 Being observed whenever you are out in public can be fun. It also can be demanding. Write one paragraph telling why the princess might like all the attention or why she might dislike it.

2 The face of Diana, Princess of Wales, is familiar to most of us. She has appeared on the front page of newspapers, magazine covers, and TV. What words would you use to describe her? Our story uses the following words: *beauty, shy, fresh, enchanting, real*. List as many as you can. Or you can list words describing Prince Charles. The choice is yours.

3 Being a princess might seem like being in a fairy tale, but some of it might be hard work. Do you think that you would like to be part of the royal family? State your reasons why or why not.

15 STRANGE CREATURES OF GALAPAGOS

Can you imagine a bird that uses a stick to dig up bugs? Can you picture a four-eyed fish that weighs almost as much as a small car?

These animals really do exist . They all live on a group of islands about 600 miles off the coast of South America in the Pacific Ocean. These islands are called the Galapagos Islands. Some of the world's most unusual animals live here.

One Galapagos resident is a gull that feeds only at night. And for some unknown reason, these odd birds spend several hours each day staring down at their feet.

The Galapagos iguana looks like a small dinosaur. It has a mane of horny spikes and a body covered with scales. Iguanas look sinister , but they're really not dangerous at all.

Most of the animals on the islands are not afraid of humans. A visitor can walk right up to them. Some birds are so friendly that they seem to like having their pictures taken. The playful fur seals are curious and enjoy the company of humans.

Why are there so many strange animals here? The islands are isolated from the mainland by about 600 miles of ocean. The animals have not been able to breed with the mainland's more familiar species. They have developed separately, with characteristics of their own.

One mystery remains unsolved. How did the animals get to the islands in the first place? Scientists haven't yet an answer.

〜〜〜〜〜〜〜〜〜 UNDERSTANDING THE STORY 〜〜〜〜〜〜〜〜〜

▶ Circle the letter next to each correct statement.

1. The main idea of this story is about
   a. how animals move from one place to another
   b. some of the world's most unusual animals.
   c. a group of Pacific Ocean islands.

2. From this story you can conclude that
   a. scientists will never know how the Galapagos animals got to the islands.
   b. if the animals on Galapagos are moved to the mainland, they will become more like other animals.
   c. the animals will become more fearful of humans in time.

▶ Here are the ten vocabulary words in this lesson. Write them in alphabetical order in the blank spaces below.

exist	characteristics	mainland	resident	odd
mane	sinister	isolated	iguana	curious

1. _____

2. _____

3. _____

4. _____

5. _____

6. _____

7. _____

8. _____

9. _____

10. _____

▶ Here are some meanings of the ten vocabulary words in this lesson. Four words have been written beside their meanings. Write the other six words next to their meanings.

1. _____ live; have being

2. _____resident_____ person or animal living in a place

3. _____ unusual; strange

4. _____ a large climbing lizard found in the tropics

5. _____mane_____ on horses and lions, the long hair growing on and about the neck

6. _____sinister_____ threatening; frightening

7. _____ eager to know

8. _____ placed apart; separated from others

9. _____mainland_____ the major part of a continent

10. _____ special qualities or features; distinguishing marks

88

⋙⋙⋙⋙⋙⋙ COMPLETE THE SENTENCES ⋙⋙⋙⋙⋙⋙

▶ **Use the vocabulary words in this lesson to complete the following sentences. Use each word only once. The first one has been done for you.**

exist	odd	mane	curious	isolated
resident	iguana	sinister	mainland	characteristics

1. A group of strange animals _____exist_____ on the Galapagos Islands.

2. Would you like to be a _____ of these islands?

3. The animals on the islands are not like those on the _____.

4. The _____ is an animal that looks like a dinosaur.

5. Like horses, iguanas also have a _____ along their necks.

6. Do you know some of the _____ that iguanas have?

7. Some people say iguanas have _____ expressions, but I don't think so.

8. Most animals are _____ and like to explore.

9. The animals of the Galapagos are considered _____ because they don't think or look like other animals.

10. How long do you think they will be _____ from the mainland?

⋙⋙⋙⋙⋙⋙ USE YOUR OWN WORDS ⋙⋙⋙⋙⋙⋙

▶ **Look at the picture. What words come into your mind other than the ones you just matched with their meanings? Write them on the blank lines below. To help you get started, here are two good words:**

1. _____rocks_____
2. _____claws_____
3. _____
4. _____
5. _____
6. _____
7. _____
8. _____
9. _____
10. _____

► In a crossword puzzle, there is a group of boxes, some with numbers in them. There are also two columns of words or definitions, one for "across" and the other for "down." **Do the puzzle. Each of the words in the puzzle will be one of the vocabulary words in this lesson.**

Across

2. separated from others

5. a large lizard

6. live

Down

1. unusual; strange

3. threatening; frightening

4. hair on an animal's neck

► **Here are the ten vocabulary words for this lesson:**

exist	characteristics	mainland	resident	odd
mane	sinister	isolated	iguana	curious

► **There are six blank spaces in the story below. Four vocabulary words have already been used in the story. They are underlined. Use the other six words to fill in the blank spaces.**

The Shetland Islands, unlike the Galapagos Islands, are not _____ from the <u>mainland</u> by a vast stretch of ocean. Neither do any creatures with the <u>sinister</u> look of the _____ or the <u>odd</u> look of the Galapagos turtle _____ here. There is a _____ that is native to these islands, the Shetland pony. This animal's physical <u>characteristics</u> are short legs, a small body, a shaggy coat, a flowing _____, and a long tail. Many _____ tourists visit the Shetland Islands every year, just to see the Shetland ponies.

Learn More About Shetland and Galapagos

▶Do the three exercises below on a separate sheet of paper or in your notebook. Then turn them in to your teacher.

1 Do some research and write a paragraph on the Shetland Islands. Include the answers to the following: To what country do the Shetland Islands belong? Where are the islands located? What are some of the physical characteristics of the islands' countryside? What is the climate like?

2 Go to the library and find out more about the different animals that live in the Galapagos Islands. Then try to find pictures of these animals in old magazines. Make a scrapbook or poster and label each picture.

3 Make a list of five books or magazines that contain information on the Galapagos Islands.

JANE GOODALL
THE CHIMP LADY

Jane Goodall has a mission. She wants to change the way people think about animals. She used to write books and lectures for adults. Now she is writing books for children. "If we can't get messages to children about animals," she says, "forget about the natural world, because the children of today are going to be the grown-ups of tomorrow."

Goodall has spent much of her life in the African jungle where she studies chimpanzees, the closest species to humans . She wants to share her love of chimpanzees with young people. "I want to give kids an understanding and awareness of the wonder of animals," she says. Sometimes, her mission has led her to strange behavior . Almost all the children who talk to her remember that she eats bugs! She does it to show the chimps that she is like them. It may sound disgusting , but it has helped her to gain the chimp's trust . That trust has led to important new knowledge of these wonderful animals.

For her research Goodall needs few tools : a pencil, a notebook, a tape recorder, and a camera. However, she wasn't trained to be a scientist. She says she had a desire for knowledge, but she also cares very much for the animals she studies. She insists they have personalities , just like people. "Animals have their own needs, emotions , and feelings," she says. "They matter."

〰〰〰〰〰〰〰〰〰 **UNDERSTANDING THE STORY** 〰〰〰〰〰〰〰〰〰

▶ **Circle the letter next to each correct statement.**

1. The main idea of this story is:
   a. Jane Goodall wants to live in the jungle.
   b. Jane Goodall wants children to learn about chimpanzees.
   c. Jane Goodall thinks chimpanzees can help people.

2. Even though it doesn't say so in the story, you can tell that Jane Goodall:
   a. likes chimpanzees.
   b. has studied in Africa.
   c. does not think adults understand about animals.

▶Here are the ten vocabulary words in this lesson. Write them in alphabetical order in the blank spaces below.

lectures	messages	humans	awareness	behavior
disgusting	trust	tools	personalities	emotions

1. _____   6. _____

2. _____   7. _____

3. _____   8. _____

4. _____   9. _____

5. _____   10. _____

☙☙☙☙☙☙☙☙☙ WHAT DO THE WORDS MEAN? ☙☙☙☙☙☙☙☙☙

▶Here are some meanings of the ten vocabulary words in this lesson. Four words have been written beside their meanings. Write the other six words next to their meanings.

1. _____ making one feel sick

2. _____tools_____ equipment

3. _____ feelings such as happiness or sadness

4. _____messages_____ most important ideas

5. _____ speeches

6. _____awareness_____ knowledge

7. _____ actions or conduct

8. _____personalities_____ individual identities

9. _____ people

10. _____ confidence or faith

94

▶Use the vocabulary words in this lesson to complete the following sentences. Use each word only once. The first one has been done for you.

lectures	messages	humans	awareness	behavior
disgusting	trust	tools	personalities	emotions

1. Many scientists have begun to study animals: they hope to build an _____awareness_____ of the importance of nature.

2. Scientists may study chimps or whales so they can learn more about _____ and the life of people.

3. You might need simple _____, such as a notebook and cameras.

4. First, you must gain the _____ of the animals you will study.

5. Their _____ must be copied, so you do not frighten them.

6. Some actions, such as eating bugs, may seem _____.

7. All the animals have individual _____.

8. Many animals have _____ such as happiness, just like humans.

9. Later, you may want to give _____ to people who want to know more about your animals.

10. You will want them to get _____, such as "save the animals."

▶Look at the picture. What words come into your mind other than the ones you have learned in this story? Write them on the blank lines below. To help you get started, here are two good words:

1. _____kind_____
2. _____intelligent_____
3. _____
4. _____
5. _____
6. _____
7. _____
8. _____
9. _____
10. _____

▶The story you just read has many interesting words that were not underlined as vocabulary words. Six of these words are listed below. Can you think of a synonym for each of these words? Remember, a **synonym** is a word that means the same, or nearly the same, as another word. *Joyful* and *happy* are synonyms. **Write the synonyms in the blank space next to the word.**

1. mission _____

2. children _____

3. research _____

4. trained _____

5. caring _____

6. species _____

▶**Here are the ten vocabulary words for this lesson:**

lectures	messages	humans	awareness	behavior
disgusting	trust	tools	personalities	emotions

▶**There are six blank spaces in the story below. Four vocabulary words have already been used in the story. They are underlined. Use the other six words to fill in the blank spaces.**

We must build an _____ of the importance of wild animals. It is really _____ how people have killed and injured these animals. This <u>behavior</u> makes no sense to intelligent people. How can we gain the _____ of the animals if they are afraid people will harm them?

It is the responsibility of <u>humans</u> to learn about these animals. We must study their _____ so we can learn to help them survive. It doesn't take expensive _____ to protect animals. We must act on our <u>emotions</u> and show them that we care about them.

We might try _____ to interested audiences, or television programs. We must get these <u>messages</u> to people in time to save the animals!

Learn More About Wild Animals

▶ Do the three exercises below on a separate sheet of paper or in your notebook. Then turn them in to your teacher.

1 Animals that have almost disappeared are called "endangered species." Find out about some of these animals. Make a list telling the kind of animal, where it can still be found, and what can be done to protect it.

2 We often see chimps on television and in movies. Usually these chimps are "acting" like people. Find out how chimps live in the wild. Write a paragraph describing the life of a group of chimps in the African jungle.

3 What might you and your classmates do to help the endangered species? Design a poster that will make people more aware of the dangers to these animals. Your poster should be colorful and may contain a message telling people how they can save these animals.

17 SONGS FROM THE HEART

From songwriter to famous singer to activist—that's the story of
Willie Nelson. For a long time the public did not even know Willie
Nelson. He devoted most of his attention to the writing of songs.
Willie let others sing his words. In fact, some of his songs have been
sung by many familiar artists . They include Elvis Presley,
Bob Dylan, and Stevie Wonder.

Willie's first big singing success came after years of song
writing. His album, "Phases and Stages," was the start of his new
career. The combination of his down-to-earth language and his
creative music made Willie Nelson a popular artist.

Willie owes his fame to hard work and sacrifice . At an early
age, he proclaimed his interest in music. He loved to write songs.
He turned out volumes of tunes. Then in the mid-1970s, he hit it
big with "Night Life." That song sold over 30 million copies.
Seventy singers recorded it. Other best-selling albums by Willie
Nelson are "Red Headed Stranger" and "Wanted: The Outlaws."

Willie's latest accomplishment is in the political world. He
organized Farm Aid, a benefit concert to help American farmers in
danger of losing their land. The auditorium was filled to capacity,
and all the money from tickets and donations went to farmers in
need of help. His work has been a success in helping many farmers
and their families. Willie is a legendary musician, and he is also
willing to use his gifts to help others.

꧁꧁꧁꧁꧁꧁꧁꧁ UNDERSTANDING THE STORY ꧁꧁꧁꧁꧁꧁꧁꧁

▶Circle the letter next to each correct statement.

1. Another good title for this story might be:
   a. "From Words to Songs"
   b. "Young Man with a Guitar"
   c. "Life in the Music World"

2. Even though it doesn't say it in the story, you get the feeling that Willie Nelson
   a. would rather be a movie star.
   b. would be happier if other people sang his songs.
   c. would rather sing his own songs.

▶ Here are the ten vocabulary words in this lesson. Write them in alphabetical order in the blank spaces below.

auditoriums	public	volumes	attention	familiar
proclaimed	artists	sacrifice	owes	language

1. _____   6. _____

2. _____   7. _____

3. _____   8. _____

4. _____   9. _____

5. _____   10. _____

▶ Here are some meanings of the ten vocabulary words in this lesson. Four words have been written beside their meanings. Write the other six words next to their meanings.

1. _____ people with creative talent

2. _____proclaimed_____ spoke publicly; announced

3. _____ the general mass of people

4. _____ words used by a group, a people, or a nation to communicate

5. _____sacrifice_____ something given up

6. _____ large rooms used for special events

7. _____ in debt to

8. _____volumes_____ large amounts; a great many; books

9. _____familiar_____ generally known; recognizable

10. _____ time and energy given to a task

100

▶Use the vocabulary words in this lesson to complete the following sentences. Use each word only once. The first one has been done for you.

attention	familiar	public	language	auditoriums
proclaimed	artists	owes	volumes	sacrifice

1. You sometimes have to make a _____sacrifice_____ to get what you want.

2. All the _____ were filled wherever Willie Nelson performed.

3. Willie _____ that he didn't care who sang his songs as long as they were sung.

4. The young singer said he _____ a great deal to the old-time gospel singers.

5. The words to the songs were _____ to the audience so they sang along.

6. The audience paid careful _____ to the new lyrics.

7. All of Willie Nelson's songs would take up _____ .

8. Willie Nelson's songs speak a _____ familiar to most people.

9. No matter how many times you perform in _____ , you still feel nervous when you step on stage.

10. Fellow _____ gladly performed when Willie received a music award.

▶Look at the picture. What words come into your mind other than the ten vocabulary words used in this lesson? Write them on the blank lines below. To help you get started, here are two good words:

1. _____braids_____

2. _____friendly_____

3. _____

4. _____

5. _____

6. _____

7. _____

8. _____

9. _____

10. _____

ᴡᴡᴡᴡᴡᴡ UNSCRAMBLE THE "NONSENSE" WORDS ᴡᴡᴡᴡᴡᴡ

▶Each nonsense word contains all the letters in one of the vocabulary words for this lesson. Can you unscramble them? Write your answers in the blanks on the right. The first one has been done for you.

Nonsense Words	Vocabulary Words	Nonsense Words	Vocabulary Words
1. notntatei	attention	6. nageaulg	_____
2. satsitr	_____	7. weos	_____
3. roaipclmde	_____	8. mialfari	_____
4. clbpiu	_____	9. eovmusl	_____
5. rifsaicec	_____	10. darumiuitos	_____

ᴡᴡᴡᴡᴡᴡᴡᴡᴡᴡ COMPLETE THE STORY ᴡᴡᴡᴡᴡᴡᴡᴡᴡᴡ

▶Here are the ten vocabulary words for this lesson:

attention	public	artists	familiar	volumes
language	sacrifice	proclaimed	owes	auditoriums

▶There are six blank spaces in the story below. Four vocabulary words have already been used in the story. They are underlined. Use the other six words to fill in the blank spaces.

Willie Nelson is another rags-to-riches story. It took years of hard work to get the _____ of the public. While other artists were becoming _____ names, Willie was writing songs. It seems that he wrote volumes of songs before people began to know his name. But the song "Night Life" changed everything. Peopled loved the _____ of the song. They could sense the _____ made by Willie on his way to fame.

Willie once _____ that music was his life. Everything he has in life he _____ to his music, and he has used his music to help farmers. Auditoriums are filled wherever he performs.

102

Learn More About Country and Western Music

▶ Do the three exercises below on a separate sheet of paper or in your notebook. Then turn them in to your teacher.

1 Willie Nelson decided that it was important to help farmers who were in danger of losing all their land. What do you think the government could do to help farmers?

2 Prepare your own country and western "Hall of Fame." List the names of those people you would place in the Hall. Write the name of at least one song made famous by each of these people.

3 Some years ago there was a very popular movie called *Coal Miner's Daughter*. It was the life story of one of the best-loved country and western singers. Do you know who she is? If not, do some research on this topic. List some details about her life.

LIFE IN THE DESERT

How would you describe a desert? Would you describe it as a hot, barren wasteland? Do you picture it as a vast, empty, dead place—miles and miles of rolling sand dunes roasting under a torrid sun?

In a way, you'd be right. The desert environment is harsh. Very little precipitation falls, making plant life scarce. The temperature can be as high as 120 degrees Fahrenheit in the daytime and as low as 30 degrees at night.

But the desert is not empty, nor is it dead. Life goes on, despite the severe conditions. The animals that inhabit the desert have learned to adapt to the environment.

Since the climate is arid, desert animals have to get along on very little water. The rattlesnake, coyote, and bobcat feed on small animals, which provide them with water. The small animals eat seeds to get water. During the daytime, most desert animals burrow into the ground to escape from the hot sun.

The bodies of many desert animals are well-suited to the environment. Their skin is thick to keep out the heat of day and the chill of night. Their skin can also retain moisture. The coloring of many desert animals is perfect camouflage for hiding. They can blend into the surroundings, making it hard for their enemies to see them.

The desert is not as empty as you might think. It's alive with a world all its own.

~~~~~~~~~~~~~~~ **UNDERSTANDING THE STORY** ~~~~~~~~~~~~~~~

▶**Circle the letter next to each correct statement.**

1. This story is mainly about
   a. the geography of the desert.
   b. how animals survive in the desert.
   c. the climate of the desert.

2. From this story, you can conclude that
   a. not all animals could live in the desert.
   b. life in the desert is not very difficult.
   c. the climate of the desert is changing.

▶ Here are the ten vocabulary words in this lesson. Write them in alphabetical order in the blank spaces below.

describe	retain	environment	burrow	arid
camouflage	torrid	precipitation	inhabit	adapt

1._____

2._____

3._____

4._____

5._____

6._____

7._____

8._____

9._____

10._____

▶ Here are some meanings of the ten vocabulary words in this lesson. Four words have been written beside their meanings. Write the other six words next to their meanings.

1._____describe_____ tell about in words

2._____ very hot

3._____environment_____ surrounding conditions or influences

4._____ live or dwell in

5._____ make fit or suitable; adjust

6._____ without water; dry

7._____ dig a hole in the ground; tunnel

8._____precipitation_____ rain, snow, sleet, hail, or mist

9._____ hold or keep in

10._____camouflage_____ any disguise that hides or protects

106

≈≈≈≈≈≈≈≈≈≈≈ COMPLETE THE SENTENCES ≈≈≈≈≈≈≈≈≈≈≈

▶ Use the vocabulary words in this lesson to complete the following sentences. Use each word only once. The first one has been done for you.

describe	retain	environment	burrow	arid
camouflage	torrid	precipitation	inhabit	adapt

1. What color are animals who _____camouflage_____ themselves in the desert?

2. The _____ sand blew in our faces and made it difficult to walk in the desert.

3. I hope I can _____ the memory of our trip to the Sahara Desert.

4. The _____ of the desert is not one I could stand for very long.

5. In his story he tried to _____ the Mojave Desert on a hot August afternoon.

6. Use your library to learn which animals _____ the desert.

7. Would you choose to live in a moist or an _____ climate?

8. Desert animals have to _____ into the earth or they will die from the heat of the sun.

9. In order to make all the plants grow, jungles have much more _____ than the desert.

10. To survive in difficult climates, animals must _____ or they will die.

≈≈≈≈≈≈≈≈≈≈≈ USE YOUR OWN WORDS ≈≈≈≈≈≈≈≈≈≈≈

▶ Look at the picture. What words come into your mind other than the ones you just matched with their meanings? Write them on the blank lines below. To help you get started, here are two good words:

1. _____horizon_____
2. _____hot_____
3. _____
4. _____
5. _____
6. _____
7. _____
8. _____
9. _____
10. _____

▶In each of the following lists of words, one word is out of place. Circle that word. You may use your dictionary.

1. burrow   dig   tunnel   excavate   discourage

2. retain   keep   hold   save   lose

3. arid   dry   parched   damp   desertlike

4. camouflage   disguise   conceal   reveal   hide

5. adapt   conform   habit   adjust   fit

▶Here are the ten vocabulary words for this lesson:

describe	retain	environment	burrow	arid
camouflage	torrid	precipitation	inhabit	adapt

▶There are six blank spaces in the story below. Four vocabulary words have already been used in the story. They are underlined. Use the other six words to fill in the blank spaces.

A _____ sun bakes the land with temperatures of over 120 degrees. At night, because this land does not <u>retain</u> heat, the temperature drops to 30 degrees or less. Many animals _____ into the <u>arid</u> ground or crawl under rocks to escape the heat of the day. The creatures that _____ this desolate place must _____ to living in a land with little or no _____. Nature has helped some animals by making their skin or pelt an almost perfect _____ to hide them from their enemies. Anyone who has been in the desert would <u>describe</u> it as a most difficult <u>environment</u> in which to live.

108

Learn More About Environment

▶Do the three exercises below on a separate sheet of paper or in your notebook. Then turn them in to your teacher.

1 The Arctic tundra is another "barren wasteland." Find out about it and write several sentences describing it.

2 The safeguarding of our environment has become a major concern of most people. Find out about an environmental problem in your locality. Describe the problem and give your thoughts on how the problem might be solved.

3 Can you name five desert animals that are not mentioned in the story? Ask your librarian for help, if you need it.

The largest theater in ancient Rome was the Colosseum. Built 19 centuries ago, it had a seating capacity of 45,000. (Just compare that to the Houston Astrodome, which holds 50,000.)

The Colosseum was four stories high. The seats inside were made of marble. A wall separated the audience from the arena where the entertainments took place.

We can learn something about the ancient Romans from the kinds of shows they liked. They must have been very cruel. Some of their "games" would be illegal today.

The Romans went to the Colosseum to watch wild animals fighting. Other popular shows were chariot races and sea battles.

In the early days of the Colosseum, it was possible to flood the arena. Full-sized boats were brought in, and a mock battle was fought while the people cheered for their favorite ships.

The Romans also loved to watch gladiators fight. The original gladiators were prisoners of war, slaves, or criminals. Later, free men and even women fought, often for money.

When the show first started, the gladiators used wooden swords. Then, at a signal, they took up real arms and paired off for some serious fighting.

Often, the loser's fate was in the audience's hands. If a majority of the people waved their handkerchiefs, he was spared.

Some critics say that TV may turn us into violent people. What do you think? Would you enjoy an afternoon at the Colosseum with the ancient Romans?

UNDERSTANDING THE STORY

▶ Circle the letter next to each correct statement.

1. Another good title for this story might be:
   a. "The Great Arenas"
   b. "Popular Shows"
   c. "Games of the Ancient Romans"

2. Even though it doesn't say it in the story, you can tell that
   a. some losing gladiators were killed.
   b. some ancient sports would be illegal today.
   c. sometimes animals fought during the games.

▶Here are the ten vocabulary words in this lesson. Write them in alphabetical order in the blank spaces below.

majority	arena	arms	original	mock
capacity	fate	compare	illegal	popular

1._____   6._____

2._____   7._____

3._____   8._____

4._____   9._____

5._____   10._____

▶Here are some meanings of the ten vocabulary words in this lesson. Four words have been written beside their meanings. Write the other six words next to their meanings.

1._____ the amount of people a stadium or theater can hold

2._____ point out likenesses and differences

3._____ arena _____ place where contests or shows take place

4._____ against the law

5._____ popular _____ liked by most people

6._____ mock _____ fake; not real

7._____ first; earliest

8._____ weapons

9._____ what happens to a person; fortune

10._____ majority _____ the greater number or part; more than half

112

▶ Use the vocabulary words in this lesson to complete the following sentences. Use each word only once. The first one has been done for you.

capacity	arena	popular	original	fate
compare	illegal	mock	arms	majority

1. The _____fate_____ of the losing player was not very important to Romans.

2. The Romans should have declared some of the games to be _____ because of the terrible violence involved.

3. We may have a _____ battle in our school to show how the games were played.

4. The Roman _____ I saw in a picture looked colossal.

5. An _____ painting of the gladiator fights was found in Rome.

6. The _____ of the Colosseum was between sixty and seventy thousand people.

7. Can you possibly _____ the ancient Roman games to any of our popular sports today?

8. Which game do you think was the most _____ among the Romans?

9. The bearing of _____ is a questionable practice in any sport.

10. The _____ of the people enjoyed watching the games, despite the violence.

▶ Look at the picture. What words come into your mind other than the ones you just matched with their meanings? Write them on the blank lines below. To help you get started, here are two good words:

1. _____ancient_____
2. _____stone_____
3. _____
4. _____
5. _____
6. _____
7. _____
8. _____
9. _____
10. _____

▚▚▚▚▚▚ PLAY THE WORD GAME ▚▚▚▚▚▚

▶ The word game begins with FATE—one of the vocabulary words in this lesson. There are three boxes under F, three under A, and so on. On the left are three key words: FOODS, PLACES, and ANIMALS. **Can you fill in all the blanks with words? In the boxes under F, all the words must begin with f. In the top row of boxes, all the words must name FOODS. Some of the blanks are filled in to help you get started!**

	F	A	T	E
Foods			tomato	
Animals				elephant
Places	Fort Worth			

▚▚▚▚▚▚ COMPLETE THE STORY ▚▚▚▚▚▚

▶ Here are the ten vocabulary words for this lesson:

arena	original	mock	majority	illegal
capacity	popular	arms	fate	compare

▶ There are six blank spaces in the story below. Four vocabulary words have already been used in the story. Use the other six words to fill in the blank spaces.

Marcus stepped into the great _____ of the Colosseum.

He was greeted by the cheers of the _____ crowd.

Marcus was a popular gladiator. The people knew that whatever his

fate, Marcus would not lose his courage.

  The games began with a _____ battle among the

gladiators. Marcus's original weapon was a wooden sword. Then he heard

the signal that meant "Fight on!" All the gladiators ran to pick up their

metal _____ .

  When the fight was over, Marcus had won. But a _____

of the crowd waved their handkerchiefs. Marcus's opponent would live.

  Today such a sport would be illegal. But Marcus did not know any world

except his own. He could not _____ the life of a gladiator

with the life of a present-day athlete.

114

Learn More About Gladiators

▶Do the three exercises below on a separate sheet of paper or in your notebook. Then turn them in to your teacher.

1 A good title must give some idea of what the story is about, and it must interest the reader. Write three other titles that might be used in place of "Colosseum Games."

2 Probably the most famous of all gladiators was Spartacus. Find out about Spartacus in your school library. Then write a paragraph or two giving some details of his life.

3 Some critics believe there is too much violence in our present-day sports, especially football and hockey. Do you agree or disagree? Write a short paragraph stating your opinion.

LIGHTS, CAMERA HARD WORK

Are these names known to you? Paulina Porizkova, Christie Brinkley, Cindy Crawford, and Jack Scalia. They are or have been famous models. They earn fabulous fees —as much as $8,000 a day. Their faces appear on TV and on magazine covers all over the world. These models are both male and female. Many men, as well as women, have successful modeling careers. In fact, the demand for male models is growing.

Models must have certain qualities . Good looks and slim figures help. But they are not essential. A certain charm and ability to photograph well may mean more than perfect features. Even, however, if you have all the basic physical qualities, more is required. Models must know how to look good under the most trying conditions. They often must mask their true feelings. They must smile no matter how sad they feel. And then there is the matter of diet. Models must always monitor their weight. Slim models still get the most calls.

For the models who succeed, there are many rewards. Thousands of men and women may fashion their appearance after that of a top model. This nationwide attention can also lead to a TV or movie contract. As a leading model said, "It all depends on the breaks ."

~~~~~~~~~~~~~ UNDERSTANDING THE STORY ~~~~~~~~~~~~~

▶ Circle the letter next to each correct statement.

1. Another good title for this story might be:
    a. "Four Models Who Made It Big"
    b. "Good Pay for Little Work"
    c. "Modeling: The Good and the Bad"

2. Even though it doesn't say it in the story, it is generally known that
    a. models spend hours under hot lights without moving.
    b. models can make $1,000 a day without effort.
    c. all models have good looks and slim figures.

▶Here are the ten vocabulary words in this lesson. Write them in alphabetical order in the blank spaces below.

qualities	trying	monitor	fees	basic
figures	breaks	fashion	appearance	mask

1. _____ 6. _____

2. _____ 7. _____

3. _____ 8. _____

4. _____ 9. _____

5. _____ 10. _____

wwwwwwwww WHAT DO THE WORDS MEAN? wwwwwwwww

▶Here are some meanings of the ten vocabulary words in this lesson. Four words have been written beside their meanings. Write the other six words next to their meanings.

1. _____breaks_____ events—sometimes unexpected—that help your career

2. _____ to copy or to follow a pattern

3. _____ monies charged for a service

4. _____ features; traits

5. _____figures_____ shapes of bodies

6. _____ to watch; to look after; to check

7. _____ to hide; to keep feelings hidden

8. _____trying_____ difficult; annoying

9. _____ fundamental; essential

10. _____appearance_____ the way one looks

118

▶Use the vocabulary words in this lesson to complete the following sentences. Use each word only once. The first one has been done for you.

figures	breaks	monitor	appearance	basic
qualities	trying	fashion	fees	mask

1. Many young people _____fashion_____ their clothing after the models they see on TV.

2. Some models earn higher _____ than the average medical doctor.

3. Good models learn how to _____ their real feelings.

4. Under the most _____ conditions, they smile cheerfully.

5. Models must diet constantly to keep their _____ trim.

6. Careful dieting means a model must _____ everything he or she eats.

7. No matter how you look, the _____ question is, "Are you ready to work hard to become a model?"

8. Without a few _____, even models with the best features don't make it to the top.

9. Her _____ seemed to improve when she faced the cameras.

10. The director said that the young man had all the necessary _____ to become a successful model.

▶Look at the picture. What words come into your mind other than the ten vocabulary words used in this lesson? Write them on the blank lines below. To help you get started, here are two good words:

1. _____beautiful_____
2. _____eyes_____
3. _____
4. _____
5. _____
6. _____
7. _____
8. _____
9. _____
10. _____

▶In an **analogy**, similar relationships occur between words that are different. For example, *pig* is to *hog* as *car* is the *automobile*. The relationship is that the words mean the same. Here's another analogy: *noisy* is to *quiet* as *short* is to *tall*. In this relationship, the words have opposite meanings. **See if you can complete the following analogies. Circle the correct word or words.**

1. **Mask** is to **hide** as **fashion** is to
   a. flatter   **b.** fool   **c.** imitate   **d.** improve

2. **Monitor** is to **watch** as **ignore** is to
   a. observe   **b.** avoid   **c.** touch   **d.** report

3. **Appearance** is to **looks** as **qualities** is to
   a. traits   **b.** food   **c.** clothing   **d.** cameras

4. **Fees** is to **payment** as **breaks** is to
   a. employers   **b.** repairs   **c.** work   **d.** chances

▶Here are the ten vocabulary words for this lesson:

qualities	trying	monitor	fees	basic
figures	mask	breaks	appearance	fashion

▶There are six blank spaces in the story below. Four words have already been used in the story. They are underlined. Use the other six words to fill in the blank spaces.

Have you considered modeling as a career? If you have, then you know there are good and bad parts to the job. First of all, there are certain _____ qualities you must have. Your _____ must be appealing. The people who will hire you are looking for attractive faces and slim figures. To keep that figure they will ask you to _____ your diet carefully. Each extra pound looks very big to the camera. They also want to make sure you can handle the hard work and still keep smiling. There will be times when you have to _____ your true feelings under the most _____ conditions. But if you are willing to stick to it, the breaks may come your way. Then, if you are really good, your fees will start to climb. People will try to look like you and _____ their clothing after your style. Then you will know that you have made it to the top.

120

Learn More About Models and Modeling

▶ Do the three exercises below on a separate sheet of paper or in your notebook. Then turn them in to your teacher.

1 For many years, modeling was a career mainly for women. Today there are some men who have made careers as models. Some are ex-athletes. Can you name at least two? What products do they advertise?

2 Models and photographers make people want to buy products. Cut out some ads you think really make a product look good. Prepare a special bulletin board for this assignment.

3 Our story mentions four famous models. Choose one, and write a brief paragraph about his or her career. See if you can find a photograph of one of the models in a magazine. *Time* or *People* magazine might help supply you with facts. See your librarian for more information.

A

abandoned *[uh BAN dund]* deserted; left behind

ability *[uh BIL uh tee]* talent

accident *[AK sih dent]* an unexpected injury

active *[AK tiv]* busy; involved

adapt *[uh DAPT]* make fit or suitable; adjust

admire *[ad MYR]* respect

affairs *[uh FAIRZ]* functions; activities

agreement *[uh GREE munt]* being of the same opinion

aircraft *[AIR kraft]* any machine that flies

allowance *[uh LOU unts]* weekly or monthly spending money

amazement *[uh MAYZ munt]* great surprise

ambassador *[am BAS uh dur]* government representative to a foreign country

appearance *[uh PEER unts]* features; traits

approaches *[uh PROH chiz]* comes close to

arena *[uh REE nuh]* place where contests or shows take place

arid *[AIR id]* without water; dry

arms *[AHRMZ]* weapons

artists *[AHR tists]* people with creative talent

athlete *[ATH leet]* someone who plays a sport well

attend *[uh TEND]* go to classes at

attention *[uh TEN shun]* time and energy given to a task

attraction *[uh TRAK shun]* something very popular which people enjoy visiting

auditoriums *[aw dih TOR ee ums]* large rooms used for special events

autobiography *[awt uh by AH gruh fee]* life story written by the person who lived it

autograph *[AWT oh graf]* signature

average *[AV rij]* typical; usual

awareness *[uh WAIR nes]* knowledge

B

balancing *[BAL uns ing]* keeping things equal

balcony *[BAL cuh nee]* a kind of porch usually above the ground floor

basic *[BAY sik]* fundamental; essential

beacon *[BEE kun]* a guide to follow; a signal

behavior *[be HAYV yur]* actions or conduct

beheaded *[bih HED id]* chopped off the head of

besieged *[bee SEEJD]* surrounded with armed forces

blazing *[BLAY zing]* unusually fast; like lightning

boast *[BOHST]* take pride in having; brag

breaks *[BRAYKS]* events—sometimes unexpected—that help your career

bulky *[BULK ee]* large and heavy

burrow *[BUR oh]* dig a hole in the ground; tunnel

C

camouflage *[KAM uh flazh]* any disguise that hides or protects

capacity *[kuh PASS uh tee]* the amount of people a stadium or theater can hold

carriage *[KA rij]* horse-drawn vehicle

cast *[KAST]* actors in a play

casually *[CAZH oo wul ee]* in a relaxed or comfortable manner

cathedral *[kuh THEE drul]* a large church

ceiling *[SEEL ing]* lining on the top side of a room

ceremonies *[SER ih moh neez]* the formalities of a public or private event, such as a coronation or a wedding

characteristics *[kair ik tuh RIS tiks]* special qualities or features; distinguishing marks

chimpanzee *[chim pan ZEE]* most intelligent member of the ape family

clasped *[KLASPT]* fastened tightly

clutch *[KLUCH]* tight grip or grasp

collection *[kuh LEK shun]* a group of different things gathered together

college *[KOL ij]* advanced school that gives a degree

compare *[kum PAYR]* point out likenesses and differences

complicated *[KOM pluh kay tid]* difficult; tangled

composed *[kom POHZD]* calm; showing little emotion

confronts *[kun FRUNTS]* meets face to face; opposes boldly

cote *[KOHT]* cage or shelter for pigeons

creep *[KREEP]* crawl; move slowly

critics *[KRIH tiks]* people who write their opinions of books, plays, movies, music, and painting

curious *[KYOOR ee us]* eager to know

D

daredevil *[DAIR dev ul]* a person who performs with great risks

dedication *[deh dih KAY shun]* the act of opening or naming a public building

deny *[dih NY]* to say something is untrue; to refuse

describe *[duh SKRYB]* tell about in words

devices *[duh VY suz]* mechanical apparatuses or machines for special purposes

dialogue *[DY uh log]* conversation between two or more persons

disgusting *[dis GUST ing]* making one feel sick

dwell *[DWEL]* live in; spend time in

E

emotions *[ee MOH shuns]* feelings such as happiness or sadness

enchanting *[en CHAN ting]* charming; most attractive

engaged *[en GAYJD]* promised to marry

environment *[en VY run ment]* surrounding conditions or influences

equal *[EE qwul]* do as well as

event *[ee VENT]* something that occurs

excursion *[ek SKUR zhun]* trip taken for interest or pleasure; a short journey

exist *[eg ZIST]* live; have being

extended *[ek STEND id]* larger than usual

F

fabulous *[FAB yuh lus]* astonishing

familiar *[fuh MIL yur]* generally known; recognizable

fashion *[FAH shun]* to copy or to follow a pattern

fate *[FAYT]* what happens to a person; fortune

fees *[FEEZ]* monies charged for a service

fiendish *[FEEN dish]* devilish; very cruel

figures *[FIG yurs]* shapes of bodies

flesh *[FLESH]* soft substance that covers bones; meat

flock *[FLOK]* gather together

former *[FOR mur]* earlier

fostered *[FOS terd]* encouraged; helped make something happen

frequently *[FREE kwunt lee]* often

furnished *[FUR nishd]* supplied with furniture

G

gifted *[GIFT id]* having great ability; talent

graduation *[graj oo AY shun]* ceremony for finishing the course of a school or college

guarantee *[gar un TEE]* promise; be sure of

H

honors *[AH nurz]* awards

humans *[HYOO muns]* people

humorous *[HYOO mur us]* funny; amusing

hurls *[HURLZ]* throws hard

I

identity *[eye DEN tih tee]* sense of self

iguana *[ig GWAH nuh]* a large climbing lizard found in the tropics

illegal *[ih LEE gul]* against the law

indicate *[IN dih kayt]* show; point out

inhabit *[in HAB it]* live or dwell in

inserted *[in SERT ed]* put into

intercept *[IN tur sept]* take or seize on the way from one place to another

invaders *[in VAY durz]* attackers; enemies who enter by force

isolated *[EYE suh layt id]* placed apart; separated from others

K

keenly *[KEEN lee]* very strongly

L

laboratory *[LAB ruh tor ee]* place where scientific work is done

language *[LAN gwij]* words used by a group, a people, or a nation to communicate

lash *[LASH]* strike out at

league *[LEEG]* union, group, association

lectures *[LEK churz]* speeches

lifestyle *[LYF styl]* manner of living

M

mainland *[MAYN land]* the major part of a continent

majority *[muh JOR uh tee]* the greater number or part; more than half

makeup *[MAYK up]* paint applied to the face for a show

mane *[MAYN]* on horses and lions, the long hair growing on and about the neck

marvel *[MAHR vul]* wonder

mask *[MASK]* to hide; to keep feelings hidden

messages *[MES ij ez]* most important ideas

migration *[my GRAY shun]* the act of moving from one place to another

mock *[MOCK]* fake; not real

mode *[MOHD]* method or manner

modestly *[MOD ist lee]* humbly

monitor *[MON ih tur]* to watch; to look after; to check

N

navigate *[NAV uh gayt]* find one's way

O

observed *[ob SERVD]* watched

obvious *[OB vee us]* easy to see

occupation *[ok yuh PAY shun]* possession of a city or country by an enemy

octopus *[OK tuh pus]* sea animal with a soft body and eight arms

odd *[OD]* unusual; strange

opinion *[uh PIN yun]* belief or understanding

optimist *[OP tih mist]* a person who believes things will work out for the best

original *[uh RIJ uh nul]* first; earliest

outstanding *[out STAND ing]* prominent; distinguished

owes *[OHZ]* in debt to

P

pedestrians *[puh DES tree unz]* people who walk

performance *[pur FOR munts]* the giving of some kind of show

personal *[PUR sun ul]* private; special to one person

personalities *[pur suh NAL uh tee]* individual identities

physical *[FIZ ih kul]* using the body

poetic *[poh ET ik]* referring to language that has the beauty of poetry

popular *[POP yuh lur]* liked by most people

practically *[PRAK tik lee]* almost

precipitation *[prih sip ih TAY shun]* rain, snow, sleet, hail, or mist

primate *[PRY mayt]* any of a group of animals regarded as the smartest

proclaimed *[proh KLAYMD]* spoke publicly; announced

produce *[PROH doos]* fruit or vegetables

protocol *[PROHT uh kol]* rules of behavior for governments

public *[PUB lik]* the general mass of people

Q

qualities *[KWAHL uh tees]* features; traits

R

rally *[RAL ee]* new burst of energy

recalls *[ree KAWLS]* remembers

record *[REK urd]* best that has been done

refreshing *[ruh FRESH ing]* makes new again; a pleasing change

relative *[REL uh tiv]* person related to another by blood or marriage

research *[REE surch]* the study of a topic to find as many facts as possible

resent *[ree ZENT]* dislike; feel annoyed by

resident *[REZ uh dunt]* person or animal living in a place

retain *[ree TAYN]* hold or keep in

role *[ROHL]* part played in life

rugged *[RUG id]* tough, strong

S

sacrifice *[SAK rih fys]* something given up

salary *[SAL uh ree]* money paid for work or a job

satisfy *[SAT ihs fy]* feel pleased or happy about

segment *[SEG ment]* one episode of a television show

severed *[SEV urd]* cut off

shattered *[SHA turd]* broke

sincere *[sin SEER]* honest

sinister *[SIN uh stur]* threatening; frightening

skit *[SKIT]* short act that often contains humor

skyline *[SKY lyn]* outline of buildings against the sky

solve *[SOLV]* find the answer; figure out

startling *[STAHRT ling]* surprising

straightforward *[strayt FOR ward]* direct, honest

strolled *[STROHLD]* walked in a leisurely way

stucco *[STUK oh]* a plaster-like material used in building

studio *[STOO dee oh]* place where a television show is acted

surveyed *[sur VAYD]* looked over; examined

survive *[sur VYV]* remain alive; continue to exist

T

tenses *[TENS ez]* becomes nervous or strained

tentacles *[TEN tuh kulz]* long outgrowths from the main body of an octopus

thaw *[THAW]* melt

tirelessly *[TYR les lee]* without resting

titled *[TY tuld]* member of royalty or nobility

tools *[TOOLZ]* equipment

torrid *[TOR id]* very hot

tradition *[truh DISH un]* beliefs and customs handed down from generation to generation

treacherous *[TRECH uh rus]* very dangerous

trust *[TRUST]* confidence or faith

trying *[TRY ing]* difficult; annoying

tumble *[TUM bul]* do leaps, springs, somersaults, etc.

typical *[TIP uh kul]* average or ordinary

V

victim *[VIK tim]* person or animal killed, injured, or made to suffer

viewers *[VYOO urs]* people who watch television

volumes *[VOL yumz]* large amounts; a great many; books

W

waterfowl *[WAH tur foul]* any swimming bird

worthwhile *[WURTH WYL]* having real merit